# ENJOY
# THE
# JOURNEY

*90 days to refocus, renew and embrace life*

Theresa Cannon

# ENJOY THE JOURNEY
90 Days to Refocus, Renew and Embrace Life
By Theresa Cannon

Copyright © 2017 Theresa Cannon All rights reserved. Except for brief quotations for review purposes, no part of this book may be reproduced in any form without prior written permission from the author.

Published by:
**LIFEWISE BOOKS**
PO BOX 1072
Pinehurst, TX 77362
LifeWiseBooks.com

Interior Layout and Design | Yvonne Parks | PearCreative.ca

To contact the author:
TheresaCannon.org

ISBN (Print): 978-1-947279-10-0
ISBN (Ebook): 978-1-947279-11-7

## Dedication

I dedicate this book to my husband, David. If it were not for your encouragement and prodding this book would not be in hand today.

I also dedicate this book to my children. You were my motivation to write these parts of my journey, and I hope they enrich yours.

Love you all!

# Table of Contents

| | |
|---|---|
| An Introduction | 11 |
| Day 1 - Accident Avoided | 13 |
| Day 2 - Adoration | 15 |
| Day 3 - Antiques | 17 |
| Day 4 - Are You Equipped? | 19 |
| Day 5 - As I Quiet Myself to Listen | 22 |
| Day 6 - Baggage | 24 |
| Day 7 - Beauty | 27 |
| Day 8 - Beauty with a Purpose | 29 |
| Day 9 - Bellowing Steam | 31 |
| Day 10 - Birthdays | 34 |
| Day 11 - Blessed Beyond Measure | 36 |
| Day 12 - Boundaries | 39 |
| Day 13 - Career Changes | 42 |
| Day 14 - Come With Me | 45 |
| Day 15 - Craftsman | 48 |
| Day 16 - Desert of Dis | 51 |
| Day 17 - Desires of Your Heart | 54 |
| Day 18 - Diamonds in the Rough | 56 |
| Day 19 - Diamonds or Toasters | 58 |
| Day 20 - Do it Poorly | 60 |
| Day 21 - Don't Grieve Past Your Day of Mourning | 62 |
| Day 22 - Duct Tape and Gift Wrap | 65 |
| Day 23 - Experience Speaks | 67 |
| Day 24 - Faith Smiles | 68 |
| Day 25 - Fear Not | 71 |
| Day 26 - Five Thousand Emails | 73 |
| Day 27 - Game Changers | 75 |
| Day 28 - Get A Sitter and Take a Nap | 78 |

| | |
|---|---:|
| Day 29 - Get Your Ducks in a Row | 81 |
| Day 30 - God, Interior Designer | 83 |
| Day 31 - Gold Miners | 85 |
| Day 32 - Growing Up | 87 |
| Day 33 - Hearing or Listening | 90 |
| Day 34 - Heart and Soul | 92 |
| Day 35 - Heavenly Accent | 94 |
| Day 36 - His Thoughts | 96 |
| Day 37 - Honor | 98 |
| Day 38 - Honor Your Father and Mother | 100 |
| Day 39 - Hopes Bridge: An Allegory | 103 |
| Day 40 - How Are You Doing Today? | 105 |
| Day 41 - How Big Is My Heart? | 107 |
| Day 42 - Marriage Nuggets | 109 |
| Day 43 - Moving Forward | 111 |
| Day 44 - My Dearest Daughter | 113 |
| Day 45 - My Grandma Angel | 115 |
| Day 46 - My Refuge | 117 |
| Day 47 - New Furniture, New Future | 119 |
| Day 48 - New Year's Resolution | 121 |
| Day 49 - One Day at a Time | 123 |
| Day 50 - Our Pursuit | 125 |
| Day 51 - Passwords | 127 |
| Day 52 - Romeo | 129 |
| Day 53 - Shamrocks | 131 |
| Day 54 - Shore Up | 133 |
| Day 55 - Slush | 135 |
| Day 56 - Special People | 137 |
| Day 57 - Spiritual Squeegee | 139 |
| Day 58 - Spring Cleaning | 141 |
| Day 59 - Stretching | 143 |
| Day 60 - Succulents | 145 |

| | |
|---|---|
| Day 61 - Suck it Up Buttercup | 148 |
| Day 62 - Surprise Blessings | 150 |
| Day 63 - Sweatshirts From Heaven | 152 |
| Day 64 - Ten-Dollar Budget | 154 |
| Day 65 - The Beauty of Obedience | 156 |
| Day 66 - The Dawning of Each New Day | 158 |
| Day 67 - The Diver | 160 |
| Day 68 - The Example | 163 |
| Day 69 - The Gardener | 165 |
| Day 70 - The Great Exchange | 168 |
| Day 71 - The Lodestar Fixing Our Gaze | 170 |
| Day 72 - The Lone Ranger | 173 |
| Day 73 - The Map App | 175 |
| Day 74 - The Master Weaver | 178 |
| Day 75 - The Puzzle | 180 |
| Day 76 - The Rose | 182 |
| Day 77 - The Simple Becomes Profound | 184 |
| Day 78 - The White Christmas Tree | 186 |
| Day 79 - Those Little Foxes | 189 |
| Day 80 - Throw in the Towel | 191 |
| Day 81 – Time to Get Up | 193 |
| Day 82 - To Spank or Not to Spank | 195 |
| Day 83 - Treasured | 197 |
| Day 84 - Valentine's Day | 199 |
| Day 85 - Valentine's Day, the Saga Continues | 202 |
| Day 86 - What Is My Father Doing? | 205 |
| Day 87 - What's Their Name, Mommy? | 207 |
| Day 88 - Who Are You? Peacock or Chameleon? | 209 |
| Day 89 - Wrinkle Remover | 212 |
| Day 90 - What is Your Passion? | 214 |
| Conclusion | 217 |
| About the Author | 219 |

# Thank you

I am forever grateful to my Heavenly Father for the grace and mercy He continually pours out over my life. He has truly journeyed with me through the many challenges and victories I have experienced.

I would like to thank my husband, my children and their spouses, who graciously allowed me to share parts of their lives to encourage and bring life to you.

I would also like to thank Charity Bradshaw, and LifeWise Books for their commitment and dedication to excellence from the coaching process to the publishing process.

I would like to thank the many people who have taken time to speak into my life. You have been a strength and encouragement from the dark valleys to shimmering mountaintops. Many of the lessons written on the pages of this book would not be there, if not for you.

# An Introduction

My husband is an early riser who loves his quiet time in the morning. His days get off-kilter if his routine becomes disturbed too frequently. This is not to say that I am not an early riser, because I am. But my quiet time fits better in the evening. I, like most of you, have my plate full before my feet hit the floor. By evening, I am ready for some refreshment, reflection, and prayer.

Reading or meditating while waiting for an appointment is time well spent. I often did that while taking my mom to a series of cancer treatments. It kept me encouraged and kept my focus healthy. I talk to God throughout the day, asking His blessing at whatever I put my hand to do.

As you read through this devotional, I want you to begin to recognize God at work in your daily life. Through the good and the bad, the silly and the sad, God has promised to journey with you.

You will see "Ponder and Pursue" at the end of each reading. Get a small notebook, or use the notes app on your phone, and participate with the discussion. You need to think about what God is saying and take steps for positive changes in your life.

I pray that you will be refreshed, encouraged, and hopeful for the days to come. Enjoy the Journey!

# DAY 1
## *Accident Avoided*

*"He speaks in dreams, in visions of the night, when deep sleep falls on people as they lie in their beds."*
Job 33:15

When my husband and I were dating, we both lived several miles outside of town, in opposite directions. On Sundays, he would swing by my house to take me to church.

One morning, I was startled awake from a terrible dream. In the dream, my fiancé had stopped at a four-way intersection. As he pulled into the intersection to make a left-hand turn, a car traveling at a high rate of speed broadsided him. My fiancé was seriously injured and appeared to be dying at the scene of the accident. What a terrible dream!

I immediately began to pray for his protection, and that God would direct his steps. After arriving to pick me up, he informed me that when he had stopped at a four-way intersection and began to make a left-hand turn, a speeding car went flying through the intersection, just missing him. Had he been a few seconds earlier he may have been in a serious accident. However, before departing from his house, he realized that he had forgotten something. Therefore, he ran back inside to grab it. Those few steps altered what could have been tragic.

What did I take away from this event in my life? First, God still speaks to us in dreams. Second, prayer changes things. If neither of these two were true, I may not have my husband today, or he may have been disabled in some way. I am thankful that God still speaks today.

The verse today encourages you to become a hearer of God: *"For God speaks again and again, though people do not recognize it. He speaks in dreams, in visions of the night, when deep sleep falls on people as they lie in their beds. He whispers in their ears and terrifies them with warnings"* (Job 33:14-16). No one wants to be terrified with warnings, but you can see that prayer changes things.

> ### Ponder and Pursue
>
> Be a listener, both while you're awake and asleep. God is speaking again and again, so let's learn to recognize it.

# DAY 2
## Adoration

*"Keep me as the apple of your eye;
hide me in the shadow of your wings."
Psalm 17:8[1]*

The phrase "apple of my eye" refers to something or someone that is cherished above all others. The term relates to the pupil of the eye.[2] The eye is one of the most sensitive and delicate parts of the body. Therefore, we go to great measures to protect this part.

You are the "apple of Gods eye." He loves and cherishes you to the point that He gave His Son in order that you may live in everlasting life. He offers you His unfailing affection and protection. To be hidden in the shadow of His wings speaks of His protection. Baby chicks need to be kept warm and safe from predators. Without a mother hen brooding over her chicks, most would not make it to adulthood.

Let's take this analogy and put a little different spin on it. Who is the apple of your eye? Is it your husband, your children or that special significant other? Is God the apple of your eye today? Make sure that you cherish Him above all others.

Take a moment to express your heart to Him, for He is the One you adore, your Provider, Creator, and the Everlasting One. He is the Beginning and the End. He is merciful, just, and full of grace. By taking time to express your heart toward Him, you will discover a refreshed perspective of who He is in your life. Cherish Him above all.

### Ponder and Pursue

You need to protect your relationship with Him. Many things, good and bad, can distract you from what is important. Take time to protect and reflect today. You are the apple of His eye. Make Him the apple of your eye.

## DAY 3
### Antiques

*"The grass withers and the flowers fade, but the word of
our God stands forever."*
*Isaiah 40:8*

On occasion, my mom and I meet for lunch, followed by an afternoon of antiquing. We both can easily spend an hour or more in just one store. If you plan to go with us, you better be in it for the long haul. What is the big attraction to shop around in old, used, and often worn-out junk? In antique stores, you will see furniture, dishes, books, clothes and much more that have long outlived their maker. Everything has a story—where it came from, and how it ended up in my hand at that moment.

Antiques usually speak of simpler times and harder work. For example, a cushion in a wooden chair was once a luxury, and a glass bowl with roses dotting the rim spoke of a measure of wealth. They speak of a time when you knew your neighbor and had respect and honor for parents and grandparents. A lot has changed over the years, but the attitude of the heart can still be the same.

In our day of advanced technology, ever-present media, and everything from microwaves to micromanagement, we can put more in one day than previous generations did in a week. We have sped up to the point that life is becoming a blur.

Take a lesson from the antique store: slow down, unplug, and see who is in the mirror. Meet your families again, play a game, go for a walk, and maybe even notice the pattern on your dishes.

### Ponder and Pursue

What are some things you can do to help slow your life down? Do you recognize the time stealers? Begin to weed those things out of your life for a little more of what is important.

## DAY 4
## Are You Equipped?

*"Teach these new disciples to obey all the commands I have given you. And be sure of this: I am with you always, even to the end of the age."*
*Matthew 28:20*

The road you are traveling may feel dark and lonely. But believe that God has great and wonderful plans for you. Don't allow the storms of life to rob you of your hope.

Several years ago, a father and daughter from our church went on a one-day hunting trip. They had hunted together in this area since the now twenty-year-old was in grade school. Once on the mountain, they separated to walk a large circle.

They had a pre-determined meeting point. Somehow the daughter was off on her calculations and walked way off-course. Needless to say, she never met up with her dad that afternoon. In fact, she did not come out the next day, either. Search and Rescue set up a coordinated search. On the third day, the daughter finally made her way to a forest service road where she flagged down a car, which took her to the Search and Rescue headquarters.

The two days and two nights that she spent alone on the mountain offered her several challenges. First, she was alone. Second, she was lost. Third, she had limited food and water. Fourth, there were mountain lions, bears, and coyotes. Any one of these situations could have put her into a panic.

A person who is panicking will not think clearly; they will make mistakes and usually walk further into the mountain or walk in circles. In this case, once the girl realized her situation, she used the knowledge her father had taught her. She sought shelter for the night and got her bearings on which way she needed to go. At the end of her second day, she had made it to a small creek where she was able to spend the night and walk out to the forest service road the next morning.

Her survival was based on her training. She had been taught what to do in every situation, and it paid off. She had hope. Though she was lost, her hope was not lost.

## Ponder and Pursue

The disciplines of our faith are not mentioned much anymore. Does that make them unimportant? If the daughter in my story had not been trained, there could have been a very different ending. Equip yourself well. Read God's word, pray, listen, and fast. God never leaves us alone; in Him, we have hope, and when we are equipped, we can move out in faith.

## DAY 5
## *As I Quiet Myself to Listen*

*"And after the earthquake there was a fire, but the LORD
was not in the fire. And after the fire there was the
sound of a gentle whisper."*
*I Kings 19:12*

As I quiet myself to listen,
It is my Father's voice I hear.
Speaking oh so softly,
In His presence, I draw near.
A peace descends upon me,
He assures I have nothing to fear.
His voice rings out around me,
Giving guidance and direction so clear.
My heart leaps for joy, and my soul begins to cheer.

What a mighty Father I have,
His love I will revere.
He holds me tightly in His arms,
Compassion and mercy I feel.
He draws me closer, and my soul He does still.
Guidance for tomorrow and help for today,
Encouragement He gives me,
His promises are here to stay.
"Father I give my all to You."
This He longs to hear each of us say.
Give your all to the Father,
He will direct your ways.

### Ponder and Pursue

You can quiet yourself to listen even in the busiest places. It is in the inner stillness that you commune with the Father. Listen for His gentle whisper today.

## DAY 6

## Baggage

*"For my yoke is easy to bear,
and the burden I give you is light."*
Matthew 11:30

When my daughter married and moved to the east coast, I knew there was something I needed to take care of right away. That something was purchasing luggage. I am not the traveling type, but when my daughter moved so far away, I was suddenly motivated. I wanted to get a carry-on and a personal bag. Not just any carry-on, but I wanted the largest carry-on I could get within the regulations.

So, that is just what I did. My bag was so wide it barely fit between the seats in the airplane aisle. I could pack it to the point that I could hardly pick it up. On one trip, my husband had to put my bag in the overhead compartment for me. I found myself thinking, "Maybe I should get a smaller bag."

Isn't that how we are with God? We carry around large, cumbersome loads. We pack the largest bags we can find, full of burdens, worries, anxiety, and fears. We wear ourselves out pulling and tugging on our baggage. Oh, we might have everything folded up neatly in our professional-looking bag, but a burden is a burden, no matter how nice we make it look.

Struggling and overwhelmed with our situation, we long for someone to reach out a helping hand. Then, Jesus, just like my husband, reaches down and picks up our bag and with ease puts it in the overhead compartment. Jesus is our burden bearer. *"Come to me, all of you who are weary and carry heavy burdens, and I will give you rest"* (Matthew 11:28).

Forget about the big carry-on bag and give your burdens to Jesus. He will take your burdens, and you can take His. His yoke is easy, and His burden is light.

## Ponder and Pursue

Take time to unpack the burdens that have been weighing you down. Jesus is ready and willing to carry them for you. Write a couple of the burdens on a sheet of paper. Then, write Matthew 11:28 over the top of the burdens. Every time the burdens threaten to weigh you down, speak God's word over that situation and bring it to God in prayer.

## DAY 7
## Beauty

*"Don't be concerned about the outward beauty of fancy hairstyles, expensive jewelry, or beautiful clothes. You should clothe yourselves instead with the beauty that comes from within, the unfading beauty of a gentle and quiet spirit, which is so precious to God."*
*1 Peter 3:3-4*

Like everyone else, I enjoy looking nice. I get my hair cut at a salon. I like to use nice lotions and wear make-up. Looking nice and being caught up in the ever-changing style frenzies in our country are two totally different things.

We are so much more than the clothes we wear. Society in general tries to set a "norm" for us to fit into. Therefore, many of us try to incorporate the new style, whether it "fits" or not.

We can spend hours enhancing our outer beauty, but if we are lacking the inner beauties of love, joy, kindness, patience, and the other fruits of the Spirit, it will become an effort in futility. When our outer beauty is balanced by our inner beauty, we will shine with a radiance that would go well with our jeans and tennis shoes as well as our new dress and heels.

Oh, and as for modesty, beauty and modesty are a delightful and enticing package when wrapped under the same bow.

### Ponder and Pursue

Don't let society tell you who you are and how to dress. Remember to take as much time enhancing your inner beauty as your outer beauty.

## DAY 8
## *Beauty with a Purpose*

*"Thank you for making me so wonderfully complex! Your workmanship is marvelous—how well I know it."*
*Psalm 139:14*

My grandma loved to quilt. She saved every scrap of material from dresses she had made for my mom and me, shirts for my uncles when they were just boys, and Easter outfits for my children.

She spent weeks cutting little pieces of cloth into diamonds, squares, and triangles. Just like a puzzle, the pieces began to take the shape of a beautiful design. Each quilt had an intentional pattern, such as a star, a fan, or a flower. Though each quilt added beauty to a room, the main purpose was to keep us warm and cozy all winter long. Every piece of material and every little stitch worked together to create beauty with a purpose.

So it is with you: every detail of your life is beauty woven together with purpose. Beauty, you may ask? Purpose? Yes, your life is a tapestry of color, a quilt of beauty and warmth. Be pliable in the hand of your Heavenly Father. Allow Him to place the pieces together, to bring out the true beauty and purpose He has had in mind all along.

> ### Ponder and Pursue
>
> Point out the beauty in someone's life today. We seldom see our own unique qualities until they are pointed out.

## DAY 9
### Bellowing Steam

*"God has given each of you a gift from his great variety of spiritual gifts. Use them well to serve one another."*
1 Peter 4:10

Do you know that you have amazing gifts given to you by God to serve those around you? Are you feeling a little humdrum, maybe a little stuck in the mud? Are there people around you who seem to have the extra sparkly kind of gifts that looks much more impressive than yours?

When my daughter was two years old, she loved to sit and listen to me read book after book. We would spend hours reading. How much could I expect a two-year-old to retain? Did she understand the story or just like the pictures and the sound of my voice?

That question was answered one evening at dinner. I dished up steaming hot mashed potatoes for her.

She looked at the plate and said, "Look mommy the steam is billowing off the potatoes!"

What? My aunt was stunned at the interesting vocabulary of this little girl sitting beside her. "Billowing" was used in one of the books we had been reading. It referred to smoke billowing, or pouring, out of a building that was on fire. She had caught the concept and was able to apply it to her little life.

As time went on, it was clear she had a gift to learn and absorb information. She loved to learn. Now, she loves to teach. The gift has grown and matured. She now has a pre-school which allows her to use her gift to serve others.

Don't minimize the gifts you have been given. Press into them, nourish them, and watch them grow. God is the gift giver, but He told Timothy to *"fan into flames the spiritual gift God gave you"* (2 Timothy 1:6). We are responsible to care for our gifts and not neglect them. Even if your gifts seem to be in the infant stage, nurture them and use them well to serve one another.

## Ponder and Pursue

Make a list of your gifts and talents. Are you nurturing and using them? Maybe you are wondering what your gifts are. Ask a friend what gifts they see operating in you. Make it a point to recognize your gifts and use them well.

## DAY 10
## Birthdays

*"For I know the plans I have for you," says the LORD.*
*"They are plans for good and not for disaster, to give you*
*a future and a hope."*
Jeremiah 29:11

Birthdays should be a time of celebration and awe. On your journey through this life, birthdays can afford you the opportunity to look back on the faithfulness of God. His power and goodness along with His grace and mercy have traveled the journey with you.

What a wealth of help and encouragement you can give to those who have not yet traveled as far in their journey. Look for those who can benefit from the treasures you have gleaned along the way.

However, while looking back and helping those around you, you must not forget to look to the future. The Psalmist David said, *"surely goodness and mercy shall follow me all the days of my life"* (Psalm 23:6).[3] You must stand in awe of all God still has in store for you. You still have treasures to hunt for and fruit to bear.

No matter how far along in your journey you have come, you still have purpose, hope, and a future. I celebrate with you the treasures of the journey.

> ### Ponder and Pursue
>
> Heavenly Father, I thank You that You have great plans for us. I thank You for walking with us all the days of our lives. I pray that we will not grow weary, but step more fully into the grand journey You have ahead for us.

## DAY 11
## Blessed Beyond Measure

*"Children are a gift from the LORD;
they are a reward from him."*
Psalm 127:3

At times, I miss my children so much. It is like there's an ache in my arms that would go away if I could just give them a hug. My ears would tingle at the sound of their voices, listening to them banter back and forth or just hearing them laugh. Just to have them near, to feel their presence in the room, would be a treat. What fun it would be make popcorn or milkshakes and watch a movie.

My children are amazing. We have walked through so much together. We've learned together, laughed together, and cried together. Now they are making their own way and doing a great job. I couldn't be prouder of them. All my children love the Lord with all their heart. I am so grateful for that.

We see a glimpse of the father-heart of God in the story of the prodigal son. The scripture tells us that the father saw his returning son when he was still a long way off. The father yearned for his missing son. Maybe he went to that porch every day to see if his son would return. At the sight of his son, the father ran to meet him. He hugged him, kissed him, and welcomed him home. He threw a great party so all would know that his son had returned:

> *"So he returned home to his father. And while he was still a long way off, his father saw him coming. Filled with love and compassion, he ran to his son, embraced him, and kissed him. His son said to him, 'Father, I have sinned against both heaven and you, and I am no longer worthy of being called your son.'*
>
> *But his father said to the servants, 'Quick! Bring the finest robe in the house and put it on him. Get a ring for his finger and sandals for his feet. And kill the calf we have been fattening. We must celebrate with a feast, for this son of mine was dead and has now returned to life. He was lost, but now he is found.' So the party began."*
> (Luke 15:20-24)

Whatever stage your family is at, children are a gift from God. Some of you may not have children of your own, but have adopted in your heart nieces, nephews, siblings, or others that you would love to hold close again. I may miss my children on occasion, but I am pleased that they are who they are, doing what they feel God has put in their hearts to do. I am truly blessed beyond measure. So are you!

> ### Ponder and Pursue
>
> Count your blessings. I have a page in my journal that is titled "I Am Thankful For…" Make this a page in your journal and begin listing everything you are thankful for. I have a wide variety on my list, from faith and family to a hot shower and a glass of iced tea.

## DAY 12
### Boundaries

*"When Moses' father-in-law saw all that Moses was doing for the people, he asked, 'What are you really accomplishing here? Why are you trying to do all this alone while everyone stands around you from morning till evening?'"*
Exodus 18:14

Moses' father-in-law confronted Moses for allowing himself to be rundown and overwhelmed. What are you accomplishing when you do all the work by yourself while everyone is standing around watching? That is a good question. Many of you could relate to Moses. A lot needs done every day. Whether you work at home or outside of the home, the to-do list is overwhelming. It also seems there is always a horde of people ready to add one more thing to the list.

What is a person to do? It can be hard to tell someone no. It is so hard, in fact, that the yes pile may begin to rule your life. You find yourself bouncing from one commitment to another, barely in time to grab a bite to eat on the way.

Take a look at your life, and begin evaluating. What is at the core of my life? Am I married, do I have children, do I have a job outside the home or a home business? Is there any time in my day for me? Ever? Do I have commitments to church, charities, and civic events?

Once you determine what your core values are, are you making them a priority? Do they get the best from you? Do you feel you can add some extra commitments to your plate? Be choosy. This is like changing your eating habits. Maybe you will not have a candy bar every day at 3:00 anymore. Maybe you will need to say no to a few activities or events at this time in your life. You are ever-changing. What you may have to say no to today, you may be able to say yes to six months or a year from now.

What are you really accomplishing here? Make it count. It is okay to back away from some things for a season, so that you may fully embrace the priorities in your life right now. Don't forget to put a little "me time" on your plate.

## Ponder and Pursue

Boundaries are a good thing. If you didn't have a backyard fence, the dog would run off and your children would be over bugging the neighbors. Not to mention, the neighbors' dog is now over at your house, and you are not sure who is sleeping in the hammock. It is okay to have boundaries or build fences. You can always tear them out later or put in a gate.

## DAY 13

## Career Changes

*"For everything there is a season, a time for
every activity under heaven."*
*Ecclesiastes 3:1*

I heard the term "career mom" a few weeks ago with a little twist on the traditional definition. This time, it was referring to a mom who made a career of being a mom—a mom whose main identity was being a mom.

I know a lady who, outside of her small part time job, spent all her time raising her two children. She was involved in their school, after-school activities, church, etc. She dedicated her life to being a great mom. Then one day, the children graduated, and together they moved to another state to take advantage of new opportunities. Unfortunately, it was a long way from home.

The children did very well—excitement, adventure and opportunities all at their fingertips. Mom, on the other hand, was now left with no one to take care of. Not that she wanted to babysit grown children. Nor did she want to have couch potatoes that she would have to kick out one day. But somehow, this didn't feel like the future she expected.

I put all my energy into being the best mom possible. I had a job that allowed my children to be onsite all the time. We homeschooled our children and took them to "after school" activities, church etc. So I guess I could also qualify as a career mom.

What is a career-mom to do when the children end up being confident, independent, self-starters, just like we trained them to be? We need to let them do what God has put in their hearts. We need to ask God to give us vision to move ahead in our lives. This is our opportunity to begin looking at new ideas and desires. Take classes and get a certificate or a degree in an area you are interested in. Start a new career. Maybe you would like to be a volunteer.

There are many organizations that could use faithful people. In our community, there is a food bank, thrift stores, a food kitchen, help for single moms, big brother and big sister-type programs, a pregnancy center, and the list goes on.

Are you looking at a career change? Maybe you see change just around the corner. Change is usually not easy, but most of the time it is necessary. Don't throw out your mom degree. We never stop being a mom; the job description just gets modified with time. Don't spend the second half of your life sitting on the couch, wishing things were different. Get up and make a difference.

### Ponder and Pursue

If you are in a season of change in your life right now, don't be overwhelmed by it. Begin looking at the new opportunities ahead of you and step into them.

## DAY 14

## Come with Me

*"Above all, clothe yourselves with love, which binds us all together in perfect harmony."*
*Colossians 3:14*

A young girl and her grandfather traveled a great distance for the grandfather to conduct business. Unfortunately, the business deal was not successfully closed. A bit downcast, the girl and her grandfather began the long journey back to their home.

The grandfather said to his granddaughter, "What a waste of a time this day turned out to be."

The granddaughter replied, "It wasn't a waste, Grandfather. I got to spend the day with you."

If only we could see life through the eyes of a child a little more often. The business deal may have been a disappointment, but the time spent together was cherished.

When Adam and Eve were in the garden, God came to visit with them every day, not to conduct business, or to make plans for a new gazebo, but to take time with His family. We all have need of quality time with those in our lives. Quality time says, "I love you."

Some of us need the expression of quality time more frequently than others to feel loved and cherished. Maybe gifts speak louder to you. You don't need hours of someone's time, but a bouquet of flowers will speak volumes. Are you one who thrives on time spent with family and friends? It is okay to share this information with them. If they don't know that about you, you may feel neglected and unloved.

God created us as unique individuals. We are not little robots, or in the one-size-fits-all category. Unfortunately, we don't all feel loved the same way. If we did, that would make life so much easier. We generally express our love to another person in the way we would like to be loved.

Pay attention to your family and friends and see what speaks love to them. Is it a kind word, a hug, helping with a project, spending time with them, or knowing that perfect item that would make them feel special?

## Ponder and Pursue

Think about the people in your life. How do they feel loved the most? How do you feel loved? Make a list of the people closest to you and start discovering how they receive love the best. It might even be spending the day with you on an unfruitful business trip.

Every moment counts.

## DAY 15

## Craftsman

*"I have personally appointed Oholiab son of Ahisamak, of the tribe of Dan, to be his assistant."*
*Exodus 31:6*

Are you a doctor, hair stylist or a stay at home mom? Maybe you are an author or an accountant. You are probably working eight-to-five, but how does that compare to having a ministry that reaches out to hundreds of people? Sometimes in Christian circles, ministry is elevated far above the common worker. However, God has given you talents and skills that will enable you to enrich the lives of the people around you.

Exodus 31 introduces two talented workers:

> *"Then the Lord said to Moses, "See, I have chosen Bezalel son of Uri, the son of Hur, of the tribe of Judah, and I have filled him with the Spirit of God, with wisdom, with understanding, with knowledge and with all kinds of skills—to make artistic designs for work in gold, silver and bronze, to cut and set stones, to work in wood, and to engage in all kinds of crafts. Moreover, I have appointed Oholiab son of Ahisamak, of the tribe of Dan, to help him"* (Exodus 31:1-6).

God chose Bezalel, filled him with the Spirit of God, and equipped him in every way possible to fulfill Gods plan and purpose. Oholiab also had a divine purpose in God's plan. He was Bezalel's assistant.

Would you say the pastor who is fulfilling God's plan by shepherding a congregation has a greater ministry than the carpenter who laid the beautiful hard wood floor throughout your house? You are called to minister, to share the love of God with a hurting world. You are equipped to fulfill your part of the plan. God used three people in this passage to accomplish the great task of preparing the temple—Moses, Bezalel, and Oholiab.

You do not see Oholiab leading the nation of Israel, or Bezalel helping Moses cut and set stones for the temple. God had a plan for each man, and each man was skilled and equipped to fulfill it. Each man was needed to fulfill his part. Moses was an administrator, Bezalel was a master craftsman, and Oholiab was an assistant craftsman.

Ministry isn't just a vocational position in a church. Ministry is what God has given you the skills, talent, and ability to do in this life. Ministry is a woodworker busy in his shop, a news anchor broadcasting accurate information, a scientist working to find cures for diseases, a math teacher teaching students, or a missionary in Peru. What ministry do you do?

> ### Ponder and Pursue
>
> Take a fresh look at your work today. Write down how God has equipped you for your ministry.

## DAY 16
## The Desert of Dis

*"Casting down imaginations, and every high thing that exalteth itself against the knowledge of God, and bringing into captivity every thought to the obedience of Christ."*
*2 Corinthians 10:5* [4]

At times in your life, negative thoughts and emotions may become consuming. They can be caused by situations you have no control over, people in your life, or even your own mistakes. I have jokingly said it is like a "spirit of Dis" comes over people. Discontent, distrust, disaccord, disconnection, disappointment, and the list goes on.

When you are in difficult times focusing only on the negative, you will eventually reap the deprivation and drought, that negativity will put upon your soul and your spirit. Some people have walked through the Desert of Dis for so long they have become discontented and disconnected people.

When you find yourself faced with these overwhelming thoughts or emotions, it is imperative that you focus on God and His word:

> *"And now, dear brothers and sisters, one final thing. Fix your thoughts on what is true, and honorable, and right, and pure, and lovely, and admirable. Think about things that are excellent and worthy of praise. Keep putting into practice all you learned and received from me—everything you heard from me and saw me doing. Then the God of peace will be with you"* (Philippians 4:8-9).

Making the decision to change your focus is not as easy as it sounds. It takes perseverance and courage. Sometimes you need to share your heart with a trusted friend to help along the way. The steps you take will be critical in moving you out of the Desert of Dis. Press through. *"This is my command—be strong and courageous! Do not be afraid or discouraged. For the LORD your God is with you wherever you go"* (Joshua 1:9).

Make the decision today to pack your bags and let the journey to freedom begin.

### Ponder and Pursue

Take today's verse and make it a confession over your life: *"I am casting down imaginations, and every high thing that exalts itself against the knowledge of God, and I bring into captivity every thought to the obedience of Christ"* (2 Corinthians 1:5).[5]

## DAY 17
## *Desires of Your Heart*

*"Take delight in the LORD,
and He will give you your heart's desires."
Psalm 37:4*

One time at a Christian bookstore, my husband found a picture that he liked. He brought it over to me and said, "Wouldn't this look great above our fireplace, only larger?" I had to agree. It was a beautiful picture, but much too small.

Later that same week we were cleaning out a storage room on the ranch where we live. Miscellaneous items and empty boxes were headed to the dumpster. A long cardboard tube lay on the pile. Upon opening the tube, we found a print, the exact print that my husband had seen at the Christian bookstore, only much bigger.

Where did that come from? Neither of us had noticed it before. God knows the desires of our heart. We don't always have to understand how He works; we are just grateful that He does. How it got in the storage room remains a mystery, but I can tell you it looks especially nice matted, framed, and hanging above our fireplace.

God is so involved with the little details of your life. The desires of your heart are already in the storage room waiting for you to acknowledge and find them. What are you waiting for? Take your delight in the Lord, and He will give you your heart's desire.

### Ponder and Pursue

Delight! May you delight, take pleasure in, and find happiness in the Lord. I pray that you will be captivated by His presence today.

## DAY 18
## Diamonds in the Rough

*"The LORD will hold you in his hand for all to see—a splendid crown in the hand of God."*
*Isaiah 62:3*

This is a glimpse into God's heart for you today. You are a jewel in the heart of God, a splendid crown in His hand. You are not just any jewel, but a diamond. God has placed in you some of the characteristics of a diamond.[6]

A diamond is one of the hardest materials known on earth. YOU are called to be a person of strength, a pillar who will not crumble under pressure.

A diamond has the highest thermal conductivity of any material. It is used to conduct heat away from the heat-sensitive parts of high-performance microelectronics. YOU are one who will protect, through intercession, the people in your life when the heat is on.

A genuine diamond reflects pure light from its large number of facets. YOU have been created to reflect the most intricate facets of God's love.

A diamond can survive intact in environments that will destroy other materials. It can survive severe physical, chemical, and radioactive forces. YOU have been given tenacity and perseverance.

> ### Ponder and Pursue
>
> Do you feel that you are more of a diamond-in-the-rough than a splendid crown in the hand of the Lord? Look once more at what is just under the surface. God already sees you polished and reflecting His glory. Be strong and persevere, you are not in this alone. *"You can do everything through Christ, who gives you strength"* (Philippians 4:13).

## DAY 19
## Diamonds or Toasters

*"Giving a gift can open doors;*
*it gives access to important people!"*
Proverbs 18:16

A good friend of mine was celebrating her birthday. She had some ideas of what she would like, but when she expressed these ideas to the family, they were shocked. They didn't seem appropriate for a gift. She didn't want diamonds or jewelry. She didn't want new clothes, or even an evening out on the town. She wanted a dishwasher or yard equipment.

Gift-giving is an important part of life. For some, a gift can tell how deeply the giver knows you. Others enjoy getting any gift. One friend of mine wanted jewelry but ended up with a toaster. She was disappointed, and so was the giver.

Pay attention to the people in your life. It is not always what you want that is important. What is important is that you learn to hear and understand what is important in the lives of your family and friends.

> ### Ponder and Pursue
>
> Giving a gift can open doors or close them. All the people in your life are important, so start paying attention today. It will pay off tomorrow.

## DAY 20
## Do it Poorly

*"Your word is a lamp to guide my feet
and a light for my path."
Psalm 119:105*

The *empty nest*. This time of life has many facets. New and sometimes scary options lay before you. It is an interesting mix of the old things of yesterday and the new things of tomorrow. You begin heading in one direction and trust that God will show you the right path.

Experiencing new opportunities can be a challenge. My husband has often said, "Anything worth doing is worth doing poorly…to start with." You learn by the mistakes you make. However, if you throw in the towel because you made a mistake, you will forfeit the blessing of growing into an accomplishment.

Step out. It is okay to make some mistakes. *"Show me the right path, O Lord, point out the road for me to follow. Lead me by your truth and teach me, for you are the God who saves me. All day long I will put my hope in you"* (Psalm 25:4-5).

> Looking down the path,
> Destiny poured out for me.
> My mistakes, God's grace.

### Ponder and Pursue

Are you in a place of change? Get a piece a paper and make a list of your options. Seek wise counsel, and bring it to God in prayer. Then step out, and remember anything worth doing is worth doing poorly, at least to start with. Fear will paralyze you if you let it, and you will never move into anything new.

# DAY 21
## Don't Grieve Past Your Day of Mourning

*"To all who mourn in Israel, he will give a crown of beauty for ashes, a joyous blessing instead of mourning, festive praise instead of despair. In their righteousness, they will be like great oaks that the LORD has planted for his own glory."*
*Isaiah 61:3*

An extreme sense of sorrow can fill your life when you experience loss. Most of the time, it is because of the death of a loved one. However, you can also find yourself grieving at the loss of other things in your life. You may have lost a job or had to make an unwanted move. The loss of those securities can send you spiraling downward. Maybe the children have all moved out of the house, or you have just navigated through a difficult divorce and find yourself starting over in life.

A friend of mine lost her husband. It happened quite quickly and left her grieving and in shock. As she walked through her journey of grief, she became more independent, self-sufficient, and radiant. Yes, radiant. I could see her beginning to bloom again. She was beginning to live life, awaking with purpose instead of dread.

But then a little voice of guilt whispered, "Is it okay to feel so good? Shouldn't I still be overwhelmed with sadness? Am I being unfaithful or disrespectful to the memory of my loss?"

Maybe you are still in your place of grief; everyone's journey follows a different timeline. Another friend of mine was having an especially hard day. When I asked her what was wrong, I did not expect the answer she shared. Her husband had passed away five years earlier, and she was struggling that day. She felt guilty for still having days of grief.

God is a healing God. Bad things happen in your life, and you experience losses that seem to knock you down, but God does not want you to stay down. God wants to move you out of your place of despair. He wants to give you beauty, joy, and strength. Don't grieve past your day of mourning. It is okay to move forward.

## Ponder and Pursue

If you are in a place of grief, please know that God is walking beside you during this difficult time. Remember that each person's journey follows a different timeline. If you know someone who is grieving, walk with them, hold their hand, and don't be afraid of their tears.

# DAY 22
## Duct Tape and Gift Wrap

*"A spiritual gift is given to each of us
so we can help each other."*
*I Corinthians 12:7*

One year at Christmas, we attended our son-in-law's family gift exchange. They have a large family, and everyone draws names for the exchange. Prank gifts are part of the fun. The favorite prank that year seemed to be wrapping the entire box with colorful duct tape. The recipients tugged, pulled, and cut the well wrapped presents open, while everyone else laughed and enjoyed their persistent efforts.

As I was watching the struggle put forth to attain the gift, I thought of the many gifts God has given to His children.

Thankfully, He doesn't use duct tape to wrap His gifts. All you do is receive and enjoy.

The interesting thing about the gifts God gives is they multiply back to you when you give them away. Freely receive, freely give. Don't make people pry your gifts out of you. Give them away, and use the duct tape somewhere else.

### Ponder and Pursue

What gifts do you have to share with the people in your life? Are you freely giving your gifts out, or are you making people pull them out of you? Or worse yet, are you hiding them? Everyone has gifts from God, so use them well to serve one another..

## DAY 23
## *Experience Speaks*

*"…but love will last forever!"*
*1 Corinthians 13:8*

A few years ago, I asked several people who came to our place of business if they had a marriage tip to share. I will share a few of the answers I got with you.

> "Work together as a team, like two horses pulling together." —**Rob** *married 40 years.*

> "Treat your spouse like your best friend. Give a compliment every day. Give a touch a day. Use gentle words in an argument. I never joined anything I could not bring my wife to. You got to take them on dates, I take my wife out for breakfast every morning,

this is our quality time. There is always compromise and sacrifice." **–Blaine** *married 30 years.*

"You must have trust and honesty." **–Mike** *married 31 years.*

"There were days we wanted to throw in the towel, but you just keep pressing on, you know you will make it through." **–Susie** *married 44 years.*

A marriage is a lot of work, a lot of sacrifice and a lot of fun. You get out of a marriage what you put into it. So, pour time and energy into your marriage with a heart of love.

## Ponder and Pursue

What can you do this week to begin pouring into your relationship?

## DAY 24

## Faith Smiles

*"A cheerful heart is good medicine, but a broken spirit
saps a person's strength."*
Proverbs 17:22

Smiles are important. When I went through office and secretarial training, the one thing they insisted on was a smile. Greet people coming into your place of business with a smile. Smile when you answer the phone, because a smile can be heard. Smiles are contagious, and most times when you share a smile, you receive one back. Smiles affect your mood and outlook on life.

Scientists have found that smiling releases dopamine and serotonin in the brain, increasing the overall feeling of happiness.[7] Just changing your facial expression can change how you feel physically and mentally. Even a fake smile works.

Another test used a fake smile, aided by a pen or chopsticks held between the teeth. One group did not smile at all. After completing the same stressful assignment, each of the groups were evaluated. Both smiling groups had lower heart rates and faster cardiovascular stress recovery than the non-smiling group.

When my mom was going through cancer care, one of the treatments they wanted her to do was to watch funny movies. They wanted her to smile and laugh a lot because people who do generally have quicker recovery times. In our verse today, we see that the writer of Proverbs was divinely given that piece of knowledge centuries ago.

### Ponder and Pursue

*"A cheerful look brings joy to the heart; good news makes for good health"* (Proverbs 15:30). Let's smile today. I have used this technique on myself. Making myself smile when I felt like crying helped to lift the blues away. I was able to get through my situation in much better form than I normally would have. Resolve to smile today, no matter what.

## DAY 25
## *Fear Not*

*"He will rescue you from every trap
nd protect you from deadly disease."*
Psalm 91:3

We seem to live in such uncertain times. Sickness is a continual topic for television and radio shows. A new strain of the flu emerges every year, seemingly worse than the last. There are concerns about Ebola and the Zika virus.

Fear is a common response to such concerns. But Psalm 91 says God will protect you from deadly disease. You need to cling to God's Word and not allow fear to enter your heart. Fear is a trap. But God already said that He would rescue you from every trap.

### Ponder and Pursue

"Thank You, Father, for Your protection over my life. Thank You for rescuing me from the traps that are set for me. You truly are a good, good Father."

## DAY 26
## Five Thousand Emails

*"He cuts off every branch of mine that doesn't produce fruit, and he prunes the branches that do bear fruit so they will produce even more."*
John 15:2

Have you checked your email lately? I can honestly say that I have. But that hasn't always been my answer. In fact, at one time, my email was inactive for such a long period of time that my account was closed.

After that happened, I decided I should check it more often. Even with my new commitment, I generally had between two and five thousand unread emails in my inbox. I did my best to indicate to family and friends that if they wanted me to know something, they should call. They could write a letter, send it snail mail, and I would get it sooner.

With five thousand emails in my inbox and more coming in hourly, I decided to make a new commitment. Hours were spent deleting, unsubscribing, and filing thousands of emails. What a relief to finally get to the end of the list.

Purging or pruning is a good and healthy procedure. Notice I did not say fun or pleasurable. However, the process is necessary. In our scripture today, we see Jesus talking about cutting off branches that bear no fruit, and pruning the good branches so that they will produce even more fruit.

Do some clutter control in your life today. Are things piling up around you? Do you need to delete some things, unsubscribe, or just get the scissors out and cut some things off? You cannot grow and flourish when you have too many things crowding your life.

### Ponder and Pursue

If you find yourself caught in a mound of clutter, you may need to find an accountability partner. It is hard work and not a lot of fun to declutter. Whether it is an out-of-control schedule, house or even an inbox, it can be tamed with commitment and accountability.

## DAY 27

# Name Changers

*"And I am certain that God, who began the good work within you, will continue his work until it is finally finished on the day when Christ Jesus returns."*
*Philippians 1:6*

Entering the fifties and beyond is a whole new experience. Most of the time, the children have moved out and are building their own lives. Career changes are often common during the fifties, as well as downsizing and relocation.

Some are looking to retire in just a few short years, while others have struggled with financial difficulties, making retirement seem like a pipe dream.

Many people have made changes in their fifties and beyond that have had great impact on the world we live in today.[8] Anna Mary Robertson Moses, more commonly known as Grandma Moses, the famous folk artist, didn't paint her first painting until the age of 76. Laura Ingalls Wilder didn't write her first book of the *Little House on the Prairie* series until the age of 65. At age 54, Jack Cover received a patent for his design of the Taser gun. When Cover passed away at age 88, his device was being used in over 45 countries around the world.

Ronald Reagan wasn't elected to his first office until age 55. Ray Kroc started McDonalds at the age of 53. Under his leadership, it has become the most successful fast food restaurant in the world.[9] If you are in the 50-and-up crowd, keep in mind you are still a game changer.

You can still make an impact in your own life, as well as the lives around you. According to C. S. Lewis, "You are never too old to set a new goal or to dream a new dream."[10]

## Ponder and Pursue

You are a game changer. Examine where you are in life. Are there dreams you need to dust off and look at again? Maybe it is a new dream or goal that you are considering. Now is not the time to hold back and be apprehensive. Write down your dreams and goals, pray over them, get some wise counsel, and remember you are a game changer.

## DAY 28
## Get a Sitter and Take a Nap

*"On the seventh day God had finished his work of creation, so he rested from all his work."*
*Genesis 2:2*

"You need to get a sitter and take a nap."

I was a busy mom with two children under age four, babysitting two eighteen-month-olds. I was getting plenty of advice from well-meaning friends, but it seemed to me I was falling short in being the mom I wanted to be.

One day I was feeling overwhelmed and unsuccessful, and I called in to a local radio program with Randy Carlson and Dr. Kevin Leman. As I began to share my situation, tears started choking out my words. I was even more overwhelmed by embarrassing myself on public radio.

Dr. Leman jumped into the conversation, encouraging me by saying I was doing a good job being a mom, and I would feel much better about it if I got a sitter and took a nap. I wasn't sure how to take such advice. It seemed too simple compared to how sad and overwhelmed I had become. But you know, sometimes simple solutions can be the best ones.

If you are that overwhelmed mom who needs a little encouragement, remember that simple solutions can be the best. You may not be able to afford a sitter to take a nap. I couldn't. But you can be creative. I saw one mom hiding in the pantry eating a licorice whip while her daughter was lying cheek to the floor, looking under the door and saying, "Hi Mommy." Take advantage of the children's naptimes. Treat yourself to some mommy time while they are sleeping. I know there are dishes in the sink and toys on the floor, but things will seem a little less overwhelming when you take time to nourish your own soul.

### Ponder and Pursue

Do you know a mom who is running frazzled in all directions? Is there a way you can help to lighten her load? How about stopping by with a surprise lunch, offering to help work in the garden, or folding a load or two of clothes. There are always dishes in the sink. Maybe you can afford a sitter so she can take a nap.

## DAY 29
## Get your Ducks in a Row

*"In fact, some parts of the body that seem weakest and least important are actually the most necessary."*
1 Corinthians 12:22

Do you feel distracted and unorganized? Are you generally running behind? How many appointments have you forgotten about recently? Is your life on overload?

You many need to get your ducks in a row. Some of you are super organizers, and some are not. It may take a lot more effort for you to get things in order.

Find that person who is a great organizer and enlist their help to organize you. God has made you interdependent. You need each other. He has given each of you different strengths. If you are strong where I am weak, then I should ask for help. I shouldn't discredit myself in my weakness, nor should I discredit someone else in his or her weakness:

> *"But our bodies have many parts, and God has put each part just where he wants it. How strange a body would be if it had only one part! Yes, there are many parts, but only one body. The eye can never say to the hand, "I don't need you." The head can't say to the feet, "I don't need you." In fact, some parts of the body that seem weakest and least important are actually the most necessary"* (1 Corinthians 12:18-22).

Do you still need to get your ducks in a row? Of course you do. But don't be afraid to ask for help. Or, maybe your ducks are looking pretty good and you can lend a helping hand.

### Ponder and Pursue

Look at your strengths—what do you have to offer to others? You are equipped with a skill that someone else may need, today. They too are equipped to help you.

# DAY 30
## God, Interior Designer

*"Blessings crown the head of the righteous, but violence overwhelms the mouth of the wicked."*
Proverbs 10:6 [11]

Our first home was a rented mobile home in a rural area. We loved being out in the country away from town. The landlord liked having us as renters and offered to do some extra touches inside the house for us. He requested that I go to the store to pick out new carpeting and curtains for the house. Excited, I went to pick out the carpet and curtains. A few weeks later, we received the bad news that we had two weeks to move out of the rental.

Two weeks is not long at all to find a new place to live and move, in one fell swoop. We contacted a realtor who showed us the most depressing, dilapidated houses in town. Feeling quite discouraged on our way back to the realtor's office, I noticed a cute little house on a corner with a "for rent" sign in the window.

After leaving the realtor's office, we made a beeline back to the little house on the corner. It was clean, refreshing, and in our budget. But the most amazing thing of all was the curtains and the carpet. They were the exact items I had picked out for the home we were leaving.

That event spoke so clearly of how much God is involved in our lives. Some might mark it up to coincidence, but God is personal and blesses us with unexpected blessings. Our verse today says, "blessings crown the head of the righteous." In Christ, we are righteous; it is okay to walk in the blessing of the righteous. So, my righteous friend, be blessed today because God is walking this journey with you.

### Ponder and Pursue

"Father, I thank you for knowing us so personally, and blessing us so abundantly."

## DAY 31
## Gold Miners

*"So let's not get tired of doing what is good. At just the right time we will reap a harvest of blessing if we don't give up."*
*Galatians 6:9*

We need to look for the gold in every situation. A gold miner would tell you that gold is not easy to find. It takes commitment and persistence, but if you don't give up you will be richer for the effort.

"But," you say, "I have been searching for a long time and I am tired."

That is why I encourage you not to give up. Persistence and commitment pave the way for most of life's victories. I know people who have given up, and I know people who have pressed forward. Those who have pressed forward are enjoying the result of their perseverance.

In the Old Testament, we find Moses leading the people of Israel in battle. God's instruction to Moses was to hold up his rod in victory. While the rod was up, Moses' men were experiencing victory, but as time went on Moses grew weary and laid the rod down. The victory began to wane. Moses' brother Aaron and his friend Hur came to help and support. As Aaron and Hur held up the arms of Moses, the victory was once again attained (Exodus 17:11-12).

### Ponder and Pursue

If you find yourself struggling to find the gold in your life, allow those around you to stand with you. Seek out the support you need to keep moving forward. Your best days are yet to come.

## DAY 32
## Growing Up

*"Don't let anyone think less of you because you are young.
Be an example to all believers in what you say, in the
way you live, in your love, your faith, and your purity."*
*1 Timothy 4:12*

*"Stand up in the presence of the elderly,
and show respect for the aged."*
*Leviticus 19:32*

Do you know how much you are appreciated? You are beautiful and charming, and I know that God loves you with an everlasting love.

Going through our young years can be an adventure, rewarding and a lot of fun. But on the other side of the coin, there are times of rejection, discouragement, hurt, and disappointment. I remember all those feelings. Some still make me smile, and some could make me cry. God has so graciously brought healing to the hurts and wounds I endured during those years.

Some of the situations I brought on myself, while others were inflicted on me. You know what? It didn't matter to God how the wounds got there; His desire was to make them better. As I was able, one wound at a time, I began to feel the grace and mercy of God instead of the pain I was used to. Time doesn't heal wounds—God does.

I am not sure we ever complete the task of growing up. As of this writing I have been a daughter for 53 years, a wife for 32 years, and a mom for 27 years. All those years have been rewarding, adventuresome, and a lot of fun. They have also been sprinkled with disappointment. Who was it that brought hope and healing to my young tender heart so many years ago? It is the same gracious and loving God, my Heavenly Father, who fills my heart with hope and joy today and every day.

Life changes daily. You are always learning and growing. Some days, growing up is easy and you embrace it with all your strength. Other days, growing up is terrifying, and you want to run as far away from it as you can.

But remember, God is so faithful to surround you with people who love you and care for you, people who want to embrace you with the joy of growing up. They want to encourage you to keep growing when it is too scary to even peek at life. But above all, God cares and He loves you. He loves you with an everlasting love.

## Ponder and Pursue

No matter what stage of growing up you are in, there is adventure in the journey. Someone younger than you may need a helping hand or a word of encouragement. Someone older than you may impart wisdom and courage. Remember, we are all still growing up.

# DAY 33
## Hearing or Listening

*"And the LORD came and called as before, 'Samuel! Samuel!'
And Samuel replied, 'Speak, your servant is listening.'"*
*1 Samuel 3:10*

My husband's family owns a guest ranch. During the summer, we have many youth groups who attend camp there. One of my favorite groups is an organization with a school for deaf children. After enjoying the privilege of serving them for four to five days, I observed that while none of the children could hear, they could all listen.

When the children went through the buffet line, some of them did not want to take any food, while others on special diets only wanted what they could not have. The counselor would have to get the students' attention, by touching them on the arm or shoulder, and signing to them to eat or not to eat certain foods. If the students did not want to listen, they would turn their head or close their eyes.

As a Christian, the Bible says you can hear the voice of God your Father. Samuel heard the voice of God but thought it was his mentor in the next room. Samuel's mentor, Eli, told him to go lie back down, and when he heard the voice again to reply, "*Speak your servant is listening*" (1 Samuel 3:10). Once Samuel learned where to focus his attention, he could listen to the heart of God.

The deaf students had to focus on the counselor to understand direction and instructions. You, too, can learn to listen to the voice of God when He speaks. You have to quiet your mind and all of the noise around you and focus on Him. It can be hard to bring yourself to a quiet place in the non-stop busy world you live in. However, when you finally get yourself settled down and focused on Him, you will begin to hear the voice of God. You can listen to direction and instruction. So, sit down, relax, open those eyes, and focus on Him.

### Ponder and Pursue

Don't be obstinate. Turn your attention to listen for the voice of God. May your prayer today be, "Speak, Lord, your servant is listening."

## DAY 34
## Heart and Soul

*"Work willingly at whatever you do, as though you were working for the Lord rather than for people."*
*Colossians 3:23*

Part of my homeschool requirements for each of my two children was to pick out an instrument to learn. Neither seemed very interested, but my husband and I insisted.

As a mom, I knew in my heart that my daughter was going to play the piano and my son would play the guitar. However, my daughter picked the guitar, and my son wanted drums. Oh well, I thought—at least they picked an instrument.

A few years into music lessons, my daughter approached me about playing the piano. She was doing well with the guitar, but felt like she really wanted to learn piano. Now I had to find a piano teacher. We went through two different teachers. One spent a lot of time reading notes, and the second spent a lot of time on music theory. Neither teacher was holding my daughter's interest.

I felt the pianist at our church would be the perfect teacher for my daughter. However, when I approached her, she said she wasn't a piano teacher and didn't feel she had enough to offer. I didn't know where to go from there. I felt she was the one.

About one year later, the Sunday morning message was about passing on the mantle that God has given us. This was my opportunity. I went over and asked her once again. She said yes! She told me all she could teach my daughter to play was *Heart and Soul* and mix it up with different rhythms. Whatever she wanted to do was fine with me, because I just knew she had the key.

Reading notes and music theory was a good foundation, but what my daughter really needed was heart and soul. She plays beautifully now and loves to worship.

If you happen to be wondering if my son stuck with the drums, well, the drums turned into a guitar—three of them, in fact.

### Ponder and Pursue

Whatever you set your hand to do, do it with heart and soul. It will make the difference.

# DAY 35
## Heavenly Accent

*"But they delight in the law of the LORD,
meditating on it day and night."*
Psalm 1:2

Toddlers are like little sponges, soaking up the environment around them. Soon they are making sentences like mom and running the Keurig machine with dad. Toddlers are transformed daily by the influence of their parents.

A child raised in Alabama will have an accent far different than a child raised in New York. The Alabama baby will be influenced daily by a southern accent, and it will be reflected in his speech as he grows. The same will be true for the New York baby.

By these examples, it is clear the things you see and hear daily have a huge impact in your life. As a child of God, you need the daily impact of the Father on your life. How do you do that? You accomplish this through confession, meditation, and speaking God's Word over yourself.

As you soak in God's word for your life, you will be influenced daily with God's life-transforming power. You will begin to speak with a heavenly accent, speaking like the Father and acting like the Father.

> ## Ponder and Pursue
>
> Begin speaking God's Word over your life. Pick a scripture that speaks life to you. I might pick 1 Timothy 1:7: "For God has not given us a spirit of fear and timidity, but of power, love, and self-discipline."
>
> Write your scripture out on sticky notes and put one each on the mirror, the refrigerator, and the dashboard of your car. Continually speak out loud what God says about you. Speak it until you have a heavenly accent.

## DAY 36
## *His Thoughts*

*"How precious are your thoughts about me, O God. They
cannot be numbered! I can't even count them; they
outnumber the grains of sand!
And when I wake up, you are still with me!"
Psalm 139:17-18*

Landing in our nation's capital, Washington DC, my husband and I were on our way to spend an early Christmas with our children. My excitement grew with each passing moment.

As our plane grew closer to Reagan National Airport, I watched the beauty of the twinkling lights in the dark night sky. It appeared to be millions of lights stretched across the landscape like sand on a beach. The thought occurred to me, those lights don't just represent inanimate light bulbs. Each light represented people—many people.

At that very moment there were people hurting, people at birthday parties, dads tucking in their children, people working, sleeping, lying, and cheating. There were people laughing and people crying.

While I didn't know more than a handful of people down in that sea of lights, God knew every person. He knows them intimately. His thoughts towards them outnumber the sands on the seashore.

### Ponder and Pursue

"Father, we ask that You pour out Your Spirit on the sea of humanity, and may Your everlasting love surround each of them."

## DAY 37

## *Honor*

*"Love each other with genuine affection, and take delight in honoring each other."*
*Romans 12:10*

What is Honor? Honor is having a strong feeling of respect for someone, seeing that person as valuable and of great worth. Unfortunately, we see our society slipping more and more into a self-absorbed world. What can you do as a Christian to bring change into that decline?

My mom lives in a small farming community where people truly care about one another. They know when someone is sick, when they're going to be gone, or who needs extra help on a project. You will often see a neighbor giving preference to another's needs over his or her own.

I have a friend who moved into a new neighborhood. Not one neighbor came over to introduce himself. No one said, "Hi" as they walked down the sidewalk. My friend decided to be proactive. She baked cookies one afternoon, packaged them, and took them to each neighbor. This may seem like a small action, but it broke down barriers and gave opportunity for relationships to be built.

When you learn to honor others, you will find your life becoming richer. Begin noticing the people around you. Do you place value on them? Do you care about them? Are you being proactive and doing small things that will break down barriers? If not, let today be a new beginning. Take delight in honoring each other.

### Ponder and Pursue

Who can you honor today? Is it a neighbor, a co-worker or the checker at the grocery store? Ask God how you can honor them. Be bold and reach out to someone.

## DAY 38
## Honor your Father and Mother

*"Honor your father and mother. This is the first commandment with a promise: If you honor your father and mother, things will go well for you, and you will have a long life on the earth."*
*Ephesians 6:2-3*

This is one of the verses we teach our young children. Honor is a "must have" character trait we want to see instilled in our children.

Many years ago, I was explaining this verse to my children when God turned the table on me and asked, "Do YOU honor your father and mother?" Not expecting the interrupting thought, I just sat quietly, stunned, trying to formulate an accurate answer.

Of course, I honor my mother. She is a loving, hard-working

single mom who sacrificed daily so my brother and I could have a normal life. What about my dad? Was I still holding him and myself captive because of the past? I realized I didn't have the positive answer I had hoped.

My dad was a Korean War Veteran who suffered from PTSD and alcoholism. My dad passed away suddenly when I was 13. Unfortunately, the alcohol abuse had distorted my view of my dad and the honor I should have held for him.

I began a journey to rediscover who my dad was without the alcohol factor. I called my mom and asked her what she loved about my dad and what attracted her to him. I wanted to know some fun memories she could share.

After listening to my mom's stories, I began to remember. I remembered Christmas shopping with him through the Montgomery Ward's catalog. I remembered going fishing and eating Sunday morning breakfast with him at a local café, just the two of us.

Satan wanted me to remain locked up and captive to yesterday. God had different plans. Were there still negative things attached to yesterday? Sure, there were. But my dad wasn't a bad person—he was just broken. We are all broken to some degree or another. But God is our healer, our redeemer. He brings light to the dark places.

Back to the original question: do you honor your father and mother? Yes, I do! How about you?

## Ponder and Pursue

Don't let Satan, your enemy, cheat you out of your future because of your past.

# DAY 39
## Hope's Bridge: An Allegory

*"'There is hope for your future,' says the LORD."*
*Jeremiah 31:17*

There once was a man, Ian Despair, who needed to cross a great ravine. Worn and weary from many days of travel, he had only one day left. The chasm was so large, Ian Despair knew he would never be able to go down one side and up the other in time. He felt all was lost, and he would not make it.

A friend told him that Mr. Hope had built a bridge over the ravine. Ian Despair gathered what little energy he had left and headed for Hope's Bridge. Finally arriving, he placed one foot on the bridge and suddenly knew in his heart, all was not lost. He now had a chance.

Your Heavenly Father knows how important hope is to your existence. The heart of the Father assures you, *"There is hope for your future"* (Jeremiah 31:17). Have you ever wondered what someone was thinking about you in your time of despair? Ever wondered what your Heavenly Father thinks? *"How precious are your thoughts about me, O God. They cannot be numbered!"* (Psalm 139:17).

Paul spoke these words: *"I pray that God, the source of hope, will fill you completely with joy and peace because you trust in him. Then you will overflow with confident hope through the power of the Holy Spirit"* (Romans 15:13).

## Ponder and Pursue

Our Heavenly Father has built a bridge, Hope's Bridge. But, you must trust Him and not doubt His goodness toward you. So, gather what little energy you have left, and head for Hope's Bridge. It really is there, and He will journey there with you.

## DAY 40
### How Are You Doing Today?

*"The tongue can bring death or life; those who love to talk will reap the consequences."*
*Proverbs 18:21*

You look tired today. You don't look good—are you feeling okay? Wow, look who the cat dragged in!

You could have been having a great day. Maybe a little tired, but nothing unusual, at least until you heard those comments. An okay day can go downhill rapidly when you hear negative comments. Suddenly, your tiredness increases, your thoughts grow more inward, and you head to a mirror to see what others are commenting on.

I am not saying you should not be concerned about people, but you should guard your words. Be encouraging when you ask how they are doing. Don't just steamroll over people and leave them lying there. Engage to transform. If they are sick, maybe they should go home. If they are struggling with life, they need encouragement.

Think twice before you tell someone how bad he or she looks. Our words have the power of life and death. Spread some life today.

> **Ponder and Pursue**
>
> Watch for people in your path that need words of life. Encourage one another today.

## DAY 41

# How Big Is My Heart?

*"Long ago the LORD said to Israel: "I have loved you, my people, with an everlasting love. With unfailing love I have drawn you to myself."*
*Jeremiah 31:3*

After five years of marriage, my husband I were blessed with a beautiful baby girl. She captured our hearts in a way we never thought possible. The tangible feeling of love flowing from the heart of a mother or father is incredible—something I could not have imagined until I experienced it for myself.

With the passing of a couple of years, my husband and I decided we wanted another child and were soon expecting. As the time for delivery grew closer, I remember feeling concerned, wondering if it was possible to love a second child as much as the first. Did I have enough love for two children?

After the birth of our son, the most amazing thing happened. There was more love in my heart than ever before. The same intense love I felt for my daughter was readily available for my new son. I had no need to make room in my heart—it seemed to double in size, leaving enough room for overwhelming amounts of love for both of my children. Once again, our son captured our hearts in a way we never thought possible. At that moment, I realized my capacity to love was far greater than I could imagine.

> ### Ponder and Pursue
>
> The natural love for your children or loved ones is a strong bond. How much greater is the love of God toward you? The Bible says that God's love is unfailing and everlasting.

# DAY 42
## Marriage Nuggets

*"This is my commandment: Love each other in the same way I have loved you."*
*John 15:12*

As you walk through the journey of your marriage, here are some nuggets that will make it stronger.

- Seek God's wisdom and guidance in the big decisions.
- Always offer forgiveness when the heart has been offended.
- Never let the sun go down on your anger.
- Try to out-serve the other daily.
- Build each other up with encouraging words.
- Give a hug—hold each other's hands.
- Hold each other up when burdens grow heavy.

- Learn how to agree to disagree.
- Focus on your spouse's positive qualities.
- Continue to date your spouse.

Either continue these strategies, or begin putting them to work in your marriage. It is never too early or too late to incorporate these healthy practices.

> ### Ponder and Pursue
>
> I am sure you have heard the saying, "You can only eat an elephant one bite at a time." If you are lacking some of the above nuggets in your marriage, pick one at a time. Then, start on the next, and keep going until they become habitual.

## DAY 43
## *Moving Forward*

*"So be truly glad. There is wonderful joy ahead, even though
you have to endure many trials for a little while."*
1 Peter 1:6

Our local recreation center has a wonderful pool area. There is a "Shower Tower" for the little children, complete with slides and bubbling fountains. For the brave at heart, young and old, there is a large slide. The area also includes a lazy river, which is a good work out. If you go with the flow, you can move along quickly. However, if you go against the flow, you will find moving forward difficult. There is also a lap pool for those who are serious about getting some exercise.

Moving forward can be difficult, just like going against the flow in the Lazy River. However, a forward focus is really the only healthy option. Continually focusing backward will only cause you to digress in every area. Focusing only on the present can be overwhelming and paralyzing, so press forward.

Today's scripture will help you gain a forward focus: *"Be truly glad. There is wonderful joy ahead."* Sometimes it feels as though you are running full speed ahead in an Olympic-sized swimming pool. Even though you are putting out a lot of effort and energy with very little progress, you still find yourself moving forward. Even if you never learn to swim, you will still persevere to the end. All swimming pools have an end, just as all situations and circumstances in this life have an end. I don't know about you, but when I get to the end of the pool, I am looking forward to a lounge chair and a cold glass of iced tea. What a relief! Keep pressing on.

> ### Ponder and Pursue
>
> Do the waters seem unusually deep today? Keep moving forward—you will make it. Remember, you are not alone. Jesus is the perfect lifeguard for your situation.

# DAY 44
## My Dearest Daughter

*"See how very much our Father loves us, for he calls us his children, and that is what we are!"*
*1 John 3:1a*

"I am writing this full of love and appreciation for you. I did not want another day to go by without you fully knowing how deep and broad my love is for you.

It brings a smile to my face as I remember your first steps, shaky yet determined. Your newfound freedom is leading you to places you never dreamed. My heart swells with pride and joy as I look over your accomplishments. I don't want you to worry about the times you disappointed yourself. I see through your disappointments and struggles to the beautiful daughter that you are.

Sweetie, you are and always will be the apple of my eye. I love to hear your voice. My heart leaps and my head turns when I hear your voice call, "Dad." In fact, I love to hear from you so much, I hope you call me every day. I have purchased the perfect plan for us, and we have unlimited minutes.

You have a bright journey ahead of you. You will touch many lives. I will always be with you. I am your strength, your guide, and your passion."

My love forever and always,<br>Dad

### Ponder and Pursue

As you read this letter from the Father, hear the cry of His heart. His love is unending, and you are His dearly loved daughter. Take time today to immerse yourself in the love and acceptance of your Heavenly Father.

## DAY 45
## My Grandma Angel

*"For he will order his angels to protect
you wherever you go."*
Psalm 91:11

When I was a little girl in elementary school, we lived close enough to the school that I walked back-and-forth every day. I usually avoided one route because of two large Doberman Pincers that were kept locked in the back of a pick-up truck.

One day, I took that route home because it was shorter. About a block and a half from home, three medium-sized dogs started following me, running around me and barking. I was quite afraid and began to cry. I knew I still had to go past the Dobermans. A small old lady wearing a dress, her gray hair in a bun, met me in the street and walked with me all the way home.

I don't remember what happened to the dogs, and I don't remember seeing the lady before or after that event. I do remember suddenly feeling safe and protected. I appreciated her kindness. I don't recall her saying a word. Her presence and image are all I remember.

> ### Ponder and Pursue
>
> How humbling and honoring to know that God has sent angels to watch over us. We are so blessed!

## DAY 46
## *My Refuge*

*"This I declare about the LORD: He alone is my refuge,
my place of safety; he is my God, and I trust him."*
Psalm 91:2

Do you ever feel that you just need to get away from all the hustle and bustle of daily life? We are surrounded by burdens, stress, and demands. Where do you go when you need to get away? Where do you feel safe? Do you escape to the mountains, or maybe the beach? Maybe you seek out family or friends.

No matter how difficult life can be, you can always rest assured that God is your constant refuge, your constant place of safety. There may be times you can't make it to the mountains or seek out that special person, but God is your constant. He is always your refuge and your place of safety. You can put your trust in Him.

### Ponder and Pursue

Where is your special place to refuel or find refreshment? My special place would be a garden or a nice patio. No matter the season, God is my constant refuge.

## DAY 47

## New Furniture, New Future

*"No, dear brothers and sisters, I have not achieved it, but I focus on this one thing: forgetting the past and looking forward to what lies ahead."*
Philippians 3:13

A few years ago, my husband and I decided to upgrade our furniture. I called around to local used furniture stores to see if I could find a place to sell our old set. While talking to one of the store clerks, I suddenly felt a wave of nostalgia, thinking maybe we should forget the new set and keep the old one.

This furniture had lived through years of homeschooling, sick children, family time with cushions all over the floor, and mother/daughter nights of movies and pedicures. The sofa had even been our son's bed for a time. Once my moment of nostalgia passed, I decided to go through with the new furniture purchase.

It is too easy to waste time living in the past. It doesn't really matter if you are focused on the turmoil of your past, or have wistful affections for the people and circumstances of yesterday. The problem rests in the fact that you are not moving forward if you are continuously looking back.

It is comforting and even healthy to glance back every now and then, but you find life in pressing forward. Thanks to that forward focus, I am now enjoying a new living room set, and someone else is enjoying my old, nostalgic one.

### Ponder and Pursue

Are you hanging on to things from the past? Are they holding you back? It doesn't have to be bad things—good things can hold us back if that is all we focused on. Let's use yesterday to propel us forward into our futures.

## DAY 48
## New Year's Resolution

*"I don't really understand myself, for I want to do what is right, but I don't do it. Instead, I do what I hate."*
*Romans 7:15*

A New Year's resolution—what is that, anyway? It is when you determine within yourself that you are going to eat healthy, exercise on a regular basis, lose weight, or be a better parent, spouse, or kid.

In reality, most people break their New Year's resolutions shortly after making them. This really is not surprising, as even the apostle Paul said, "These things I do, I should not do; and the things I should do, I do not."

Within yourself, you don't always have what it takes to overcome bad habits or to establish good ones. However, if you bring these things to God in prayer, you'll find He is more than happy to help bring positive change into your life. Through Christ, you can do all things.

> ### Ponder and Pursue
>
> Are you one of the millions of people who have given up on your goals and resolutions? Let's take it one step at a time. First, pick one goal, not a half-dozen. Second, find an accountability partner. Third, give yourself a time frame to work with. Fourth, go for it, and don't give up

## DAY 49
## *One Day at a Time*

*"This is the day the LORD has made.
We will rejoice and be glad in it."
Psalm 118:24*

The phrase for today is "One Day at a Time." Are you one to over-think situations and focus more on the "bummer" than the "blessing"? *"'For I know the plans I have for you,' says the LORD. 'They are plans for good and not for disaster, to give you a future and a hope"* (Jeremiah 29:11).

The blessing is ahead of us. We will intersect with it. We are even living in it at this very moment. However, when we focus too much on the bummer, we miss the opportunity to enjoy the blessing. So, today, one day at a time, focus on the blessing. God has a plan, and it will be good.

## Ponder and Pursue

Make a list of the blessings in your life today. Live in the blessing.

## DAY 50
## *Our Pursuit*

*"There the angel of the LORD appeared to him in a blazing fire from the middle of a bush. Moses stared in amazement. Though the bush was engulfed in flames, it didn't burn up. 'This is amazing,' Moses said to himself. 'Why isn't that bush burning up? I must go see it.' When the LORD saw Moses coming to take a closer look, God called to him from the middle of the bush, 'Moses! Moses! Here I am!' Moses replied."*
*Exodus 3:2-4*

I live and work in the San Juan Mountains of southwest Colorado. The scenery in our area is breathtaking. We have often been told, "It must be amazing to live in such beauty all of the time."

It is amazing to live and work here, but in the busyness of the day,

I often forget to look around and see the beauty. I can become so accustomed to seeing beautiful things that I no longer notice them. I have to intentionally make myself aware of the scenery and the beauty that surrounds me.

God wants you to fellowship with Him. Walk with Him and talk with Him. Learn to listen for His voice. In order for you to hear from God, you will have to intentionally make yourself aware that God is speaking. You need to turn your attention toward Him.

When Moses saw the burning bush, he was amazed. Never having seen such a sight before, he had to go over to it, focus his attention on it, and intentionally try to grasp what he was seeing. At that moment, when God saw He had Moses' attention, He spoke.

### Ponder and Pursue

Make yourself aware of God's presence in your life. Move toward it, focus on it, and grasp it. God will meet you in your pursuit.

# DAY 51
## Passwords

*"But those who trust in the LORD will find new strength.
They will soar high on wings like eagles. They will run
and not grow weary. They will walk and not faint."*
Isaiah 40:31

Do you find passwords as annoying as I do? You have to have a password for every account. If you use the same password for everything, it will be easy to hack all of your accounts. If you make up a difficult password, you will most likely forget it. It is easy for a hacker to figure out your kid's birthday and the name of your pet goldfish. Well, maybe not the goldfish—unless, of course, you posted cute little pictures of him on Facebook.

When you discover that you have forgotten your password, you will then spend the next five to ten minutes going through the recovery process. Hopefully, you have not forgotten the answer to your security questions. My mom had an account with the security question, "When you were eight, what street did you live on?" She was certain she didn't pick that question and was completely unaware of the name of a street she lived on seventy years ago.

The password for today is Isaiah 40:31. As you trust in the Lord, you will find strength. You will be able to soar, run and walk. Today will have challenges you didn't expect, and it will also be filled with leftover challenges from yesterday. However, you are equipped for the challenge. Most importantly, you know the password. Isaiah 40:31 will get you where you need to be today.

### Ponder and Pursue

Maybe you should use the serial numbers off your major appliances for your passwords. At least then you could open the refrigerator door and retrieve it. Put your trust in the Lord and watch yourself soar through the challenges of life.

## DAY 52

## *Romeo*

*"For he satisfies the thirsty and fills the
hungry with good things."*
*Psalm 107:9*

My son and his wife have a cute little lab mix named Romeo. He loves his food. When I go over to let him out and feed him, he is beside himself with excitement. He can hardly wait to eat his dinner and get his snacks.

How hungry are you for the things of God? Are you excited to get out of bed each morning, spend time with God, and read His word? Okay, maybe you are not a morning person. I love the quiet evening moments I share with the Lord.

The point is: are you anticipating your time with Him? Are you excited to read His word? Do you look forward to His input into your life? If not, let's try to change that. Think of Romeo jumping and bounding through the house in anticipation of getting a doggie treat.

God has His whole kingdom available to you. I am not just talking about a doggie treat, but a relationship with your Heavenly Father. Now *that* is something to get excited about.

> ### Ponder and Pursue
>
> Set aside time each day to spend with God. Morning, afternoon, or evening; He is always ready.

## DAY 53
## *Shamrocks*

*"He cuts off every branch of mine that doesn't produce fruit, and he prunes the branches that do bear fruit so they will produce even more."*
John 15:2

When I repotted my shamrock plant, I had to pull out a lot of dead leaves and break up the bound root system. It seemed pretty severe at the time, but it was a strong plant, so I wasn't concerned. With the root system freed up and all the dead leaves gone, I knew it would flourish. The first couple of days, it was a little wilted, but after about a week, it looked great. The wilting leaves had perked up, and new leaves were budding.

Pruning is usually a messy job: cutting out all the dead leaves and branches, getting rid of bad dirt, and freeing the root system. But once it is all said and done, the results are great.

You will go through times of pruning in your life, too. During those times, you will need to remember that when it is all over, you will experience more freedom, greater growth, and abundant fruit. When you feel the pruning shears, remind yourself there are greater things to come.

### Ponder and Pursue

You will make it through this difficult season, and there will be sunnier days ahead—days of freedom, growth, and fruit.

## DAY 54
### Shore Up

*"Anyone who listens to my teaching and follows it is wise,
like a person who builds a house on solid rock."*
*Matthew 7:24*

The term "shore up" means to support, brace, or prop up.

In our verse today, Jesus said, "Anyone who listens to my teaching and follows it is wise, like a person who builds a house on solid rock." Take some time to read Matthew 5-7. These chapters are the teachings of Jesus directly for you. They will "shore you up" as you build on the rock. Storms come and storms go, but how you weather them depends on where you build:

> "Anyone who listens to my teaching and follows it is wise, like a person who builds a house on solid rock.

*Though the rain comes in torrents and the floodwaters rise and the winds beat against that house, it won't collapse because it is built on bedrock. But anyone who hears my teaching and doesn't obey it is foolish, like a person who builds a house on sand. When the rains and floods come and the winds beat against that house, it will collapse with a mighty crash"* (Matthew 7:24-27).

### Ponder and Pursue

Take time this week to read Matthew chapters five, six, and seven. You need to shore-up your life with the instructions of Jesus. When you do, you will weather whatever storms lie ahead.

## DAY 55
## Slush

*"But the gateway to life is very narrow and the road is difficult, and only a few ever find it."*
Matthew 7:14

I hate slush! Bad weather can bring all kinds of hazardous road conditions: wet roads, snow-packed roads, ice, and slush. Slushy roads are somewhat deceiving, as a small section of the road is merely wet while inches of dangerous slush lie off to the side.

Why is slush such a problem? It is not as slick as ice or packed snow. If your concentration becomes the least bit distracted, you may find yourself on the side of the road, pulled off course by the slush. All of that can happen in a matter of seconds.

It is kind of like your walk with God. You want to stay on the straight and narrow path, because wide is the road that leads to destruction. You are surrounded by distractions on every side. You must remain diligent and focus on the path before you.

The last thing you want to do is get sucked off your path and into the ditch. Although on rare occasions you may find yourself in the ditch, God is faithful to send a brother or sister to come help pull you out of your misery so that you may once again keep your eye on the path before you.

### Ponder and Pursue

Be alert today. Don't allow yourself to be sucked off course by circumstances.

## DAY 56

## Special People

*"But exhort one another daily, while it is called today; lest any of you be hardened through the deceitfulness of sin."*
Hebrews 3:13[12]

Who are the special people in your life? Is it a spouse, parent, child, or friend? You have people who have spoken into your life, encouraged you, cared for you, and helped you through many obstacles.

As you live out your daily life, sometimes you forget how special people are. You get up and do the same routine day after day. You talk about the same things and go to the same places. You can begin to take them for granted or allow frustrations to begin to cloud your vision.

It is unfortunate that you can become so comfortable with someone that you begin taking that person for granted. Their amazing qualities begin to blur into nonexistence, because at some point you stop looking for them. Write down some qualities you see in your spouse, a parent, or a friend. Honor those qualities.

### Ponder and Pursue

Are the people in your life honorable, kind, good providers, energetic, insightful or encouraging? Make your list today. Appreciate the people in your life.

## DAY 57
## *Spiritual Squeegee*

*"Now we see things imperfectly, like puzzling reflections in a mirror, but then we will see everything with perfect clarity. All that I know now is partial and incomplete, but then I will know everything completely, just as God now knows me completely."*
1 Corinthians 13:12

Have you ever tried to get ready in a steamy bathroom with a foggy mirror? The image you see in the mirror is not clear.

How often do you look at other areas of your life through a foggy mirror? You often fail to see yourself as God sees you. Worse yet, you fail to see God in you, His abilities, His skills, and His provision.

You go through times of quandary, wondering what your purpose is. Do you have what it takes to accomplish your dreams? As you take time to clear your vision, you will see God is working on your behalf. He will partner with you to accomplish the purpose and destiny set before you. Next time things are looking a little foggy, get out your spiritual squeegee and clear up your view.

> ### Ponder and Pursue
>
> Get a clear view of who God is. Get a clear view of who you are. List on a piece of paper the characteristics of God, and next to that, make a list of your own positive traits. Now you can start getting ready.

# DAY 58
## Spring Cleaning

*"Awake, north wind! Rise up, south wind! Blow on my garden and spread its fragrance all around. Come into your garden, my love; taste its finest fruits."*
*Song of Solomon 4:16*

Spring cleaning is a time of refreshment and putting away tired appearances; a time of opening the windows to enjoy fresh spring air. Fall is a time of gathering, nesting, and harvesting, creating an atmosphere of warmth, peace, and thankfulness.

The same applies to your spirit. You need a time of spring cleaning, putting off old things, and stepping into something new and fresh. You also need a fall period of reaping and harvesting in your relationship with God, soaking in the warmth and peace of an intimate relationship with Him.

Are you in a season of purging and stepping into something fresh and new? Maybe you are in a season of reaping and harvesting. Allow the wind of the Spirit to blow in and do a complete work, so you may taste of its finest fruits.

> ### Ponder and Pursue
>
> Father, I thank you for walking through every season of life with us. Whether we are cleaning and refreshing or reaping a harvest, you are there with us. Your love is unending.

# DAY 59
## Stretching

*"Do not be afraid or discouraged, for the LORD will personally go ahead of you. He will be with you; he will neither fail you nor abandon you."*
Deuteronomy 31:8

I spend my summers working at a guest ranch. The laundry room is a busy place with plenty to wash, dry, fold, and put away. I roll up bedspreads, blankets, and shower curtains instead of folding them. It is easy to wrap or stretch a rubber band around a rolled shower curtain to keep it together.

However, it is a little riskier to stretch a rubber band around a rolled bedspread. I find myself cringing at the thought of getting snapped by a rubber band. One simple solution a friend came up with was to use extra-large rubber bands. They can stretch easily over a bedspread without too much concern of being popped, while the little ones work perfect for a shower curtain.

Your life is similar. There are areas where you are comfortable with the stretch, while others push you to your limits. You might become filled with fear, anxiety, or insecurity. That is when you need a bigger rubber band. God's promises can stretch out around your circumstances and hold you together.

Jesus promised He would never leave you or forsake you. What an awesome promise! The next time you feel stretched beyond your comfort zone, look to the One right there beside you. He's the One who will never leave you.

### Ponder and Pursue

Are you feeling a little stretched today? Rely on the promises of God's word to get you through. Find a big rubber band to put on your wrist today as a reminder of Gods faithfulness.

## DAY 60

## *Succulents*

*"I earnestly search for you. My soul thirsts for you; my whole body longs for you in this parched and weary land where there is no water."*
Psalm 63:1

Succulents are a popular plant in today's market. They come in a variety of shapes, sizes, and colors. I remember as a kid, my grandmother had a variety called "hen and chicks." Her little hen was very prolific, as there was a large mound of pokey little chicks surrounding her.

Succulents have unusually thick leaves that are filled with fluid. Because of the fluid the leaves hold, they can live in dry and arid climates. One of the things I like best about the succulents is how easily they multiply. My hen has eight chicks right now, and she is planted in a soup ladle hanging in my kitchen. Many succulents will root easily. Often, leaves that fall from the plant will develop roots while lying on top of the soil.

God is so creative with His creation. He made each one to survive in a unique environment. Take a lesson from the succulent. You often find yourself in dry and arid places. The Psalmist in our opening scripture was thirsting after God in a parched and weary land. The busy lifestyle that most lead can leave us parched and weary.

In John 7:37-38, Jesus says, *"Anyone who is thirsty may come to me! Anyone who believes in me may come and drink! For the Scriptures declare, 'Rivers of living water will flow from his heart.'"* Jesus was speaking of the Holy Spirit. When you take time to soak in His presence, read God's word, and share your heart with the Father, you will find yourself being filled with the living water.

It will not matter if you are going through a dry spell. You will be ensuring that your inner-man is well-nourished and hydrated. You will be like the trees in Psalm 1:3: *"They are like trees ... planted along the riverbank, bearing fruit each season. Their leaves never wither, and they prosper in all they do."*

Verse two reveals the reason they didn't wither, but prospered in all they did: *"But they delight in the law of the LORD, meditating on it day and night."* Take time to drink of the living water today. You will be glad you did.

## Ponder and Pursue

Meditate on God's word. Consider and reflect upon it. Reflecting on His word today will cause you to reflect Him to the world tomorrow.

## DAY 61

## *Suck it up Buttercup*

*"Don't worry about anything; instead, pray about everything. Tell God what you need, and thank him for all he has done."*
Philippians 4:6

If you are like me and everyone else on our planet, you suffer from bad days, discouragement, disappointments, depression, and so much more. Now, I hope you are not dealing with all of these at once, but I am sure you have been introduced to at least one of these in your lifetime.

I was having a particularly difficult day—actually, I would say it was more like a season. Days turned into weeks, and weeks into months. Mounting disappointment threatened to overwhelm me, creating a sadness I felt in my chest that made it difficult to breathe. Disappointments are often treated as no big deal. I told myself, "just suck it up," "you will get over it," and "everyone gets disappointed."

Disappointment is a real thing. It can pull you down and hold you captive. The insensitive things people tell you or that you tell yourself do not make the situation go away, nor do they relieve the sadness filling your life.

You need to be proactive. Being proactive during a difficult season is hard, but vital. You need to redirect your thought life. You can no longer focus on the disappointment. You need to pray, focus on God changing you, and thanking Him for all He is doing.

### Ponder and Pursue

Be proactive today. Acknowledge your hurt, but decide to not live in it anymore. Allow God to heal and change your heart. Even though you want situations to change, it is often you that has to change. Get a friend to walk through this with you. Above all, plan to make a move, and stick with it. You can do it.

## DAY 62

## Surprise Blessings

*"Wherever you go and whatever you do,
you will be blessed."*
Deuteronomy 28:6

A few years ago, God provided airfare and a rental car for my husband and I to go visit our children before Christmas. Our daughter and son-in-law were expecting, and we were invited to attend her ultrasound appointment to find out if the baby was a girl or boy. We could see the baby's movements on the screen and hear the heartbeat. Oh, and it was a boy!

One evening, as we sat visiting with family, my daughter reached over and placed my hand on her belly. I felt my little grandson pressing up against my hand. My heart overflowed with gratefulness for the opportunity that was given to us and to know that God is an abundant provider.

We were also able to make a six-hour drive to have a brief Christmas with our son and his fiancée. What a blessing it was to get to spend time with them, watching them grow together as a couple.

My husband often prays for surprises and unexpected blessings to be poured out into our life. This trip was an answer to his prayer, and it was packed full of surprises and blessings.

> ### Ponder and Pursue
>
> Go ahead and ask God to pour out His unexpected blessings and surprises in your life. He has them wrapped up and ready to send.

# DAY 63
## Sweatshirts from Heaven

*"And God is able to bless you abundantly, so that in all things at all times, having all that you need, you will abound in every good work."*
*2 Corinthians 9:8*[13]

Most of us have walked through seasons of plenty and seasons of need. I had been shopping at a local department store and noticed they had a sale on sweatshirts. I called my husband over to look at the great deal. My husband's only reply was, "You need to ask your Heavenly Father. He can be more generous right now than I can." I knew he was right. We did not have any extra money to purchase even a great deal like this one.

The following Sunday at church, a friend came up to me and told me that she had left a bag in the foyer for me. On my way out, I picked up the bag and glanced inside. A giddy kind of happiness bubbled up inside as I pulled out one sweatshirt after another. There were five sweatshirts all together. Wow, I had wanted one, but God blessed me with five beautiful sweatshirts.

God blesses us abundantly. Those sweatshirts were not necessary to meet my basic needs, but they were a blessing of abundance during a season of need. This was the Father Heart of God putting His arm around His daughter and saying, "I have plenty, I am generous, and I want to share it with you because I love you."

### Ponder and Pursue

God wants to pour His generous blessings out for you today. Chat with the Father about your situation. He is always listening.

## DAY 64
## Ten-Dollar Budget

*"Don't you realize that in a race everyone runs, but only one person gets the prize? So run to win! All athletes are disciplined in their training. They do it to win a prize that will fade away, but we do it for an eternal prize."*
1 Corinthians 9:24-25

My husband and I chose to homeschool our children. For one of our Home Economics projects, I gave them a challenge saying, "Imagine you are in college. You only have ten dollars left for a whole week's worth of groceries. What can you buy that is nutritious and will last for seven days?"

Budgets are almost unheard of today. Instead the trend is to spend, spend, spend. Whether it's spending your money or time, you end up malnourished and depleted.

To avoid this situation, you need to budget your life. Tell yourself "no" occasionally. Make healthy choices. How long can you live on mac-n-cheese or ramen noodles? Some of you make a steady diet of unhealthy choices and wonder why you don't have any time or money.

Self-discipline is not fun, but the end results are fabulous. You will have a healthier body, time for fun, a funded savings account, and maybe even a retirement account.

### Ponder and Pursue

So, what are you going to spend your ten dollars on today? When it is gone, it is gone. Make wise choices.

## DAY 65
## *The Beauty of Obedience*

*"Walk in obedience to all that the Lord your God has commanded you, so that you may live and prosper and prolong your days in the land that you will possess."*
*Deuteronomy 5:33*[14]

A few years ago, I was asked to speak at a ladies' retreat in Telluride, Colorado. The retreat took place in the fall, which is a very busy time for our family business, meaning I had little time to spend preparing for my part of the retreat.

The idea of being asked to take one of the sessions was exciting and challenging all at the same time. I like to use object lessons when I teach, because it helps people remember different points in the message.

The morning I was to leave for the retreat, I was gathering last-minute items to help get my message across. After loading the last of my necessary items, I suddenly felt the need to go back into the house to get some paintbrushes. So, back in the house I went, grabbing three or four random brushes, and I was finally on my way.

The retreat was wonderful. I needed it as much as anyone because I was exhausted from working long hours with very little time off. At the end of my session, a lady came up to me and asked if she could borrow the brushes I used for part of my object lesson. Of course, I was glad to let her use them. She had brought her paints and paper but forgot the brushes.

The following day when everyone was saying their goodbyes, the lady returned my brushes along with a beautiful watercolor she painted the day before. She gave me the painting and thanked me for bringing the brushes. I believe God wanted to bless her with brushes since she forgot hers. The beauty of my obedience was demonstrated through the watercolor painting that now sits in my living room.

### Ponder and Pursue

The next time you feel impressed upon to do something out of the ordinary, or even a bit inconvenient, remember that the beauty of obedience has unexpected rewards.

## DAY 66
## The Dawning of Each New Day

*"Let me hear of your unfailing love each morning, for I am trusting you. Show me where to walk, for I give myself to you."*
*Psalm 143:8*

Lord, how gently your morning dawns into day.
The dancing and playing of each sun ray
Signals a beautiful day is about to begin.
Golden leaves that glisten without sin,
Your creation so beautiful, fresh, and so clean,
I think to myself,
Dear Lord, what can be seen?

Yes child, I see in you,
The dawning of each new day,
An eager child dancing and playing,
Down my chosen pathway.
I see you through your tears and joy,
Glistening without sin,
You're under the blood of my Son,
In Him I see no sin.
So yes, child, my creation,
You're beautiful deep within.
Cleansed and washed by the blood of the Lamb,
Dear child,
You're born to win.

## Ponder and Pursue

You are God's child, His creation, and His chosen one. You are beautiful, clean and glistening. Yes, today and every day you are a winner. Rejoice!

## DAY 67
### The Diver

*"Even there your hand will guide me,
and your strength will support me."*
Psalm 139:10

I awoke this morning with a thought on my mind, and I felt I wanted to share it with you. Grab your snorkel and maybe your surfboard, and come along.

Some days may feel as though you are walking on the water. Your faith feels full. The waves coming your way don't seem to intimidate you. You have prepared for the storm and you are riding it out. Even the mist feels good on your face.

Other days, you find yourself in the depths of the sea. You are an undersea explorer, wondering how you got here, and most of all, how to get back to the surface.

The incredible thing about God is that He is with you whether you are a wave-walker or deep-sea explorer. The Psalmist said, *"If I go up to heaven, you are there; if I go down to the grave, you are there. If I ride the wings of the morning, if I dwell by the farthest oceans, even there your hand will guide me, and your strength will support me"* (Psalm 139:8-10).

Which is the greatest miracle: walking on the waves, or the having the breath to explore the depths of the sea? Both are an extension of God's great love for you. Whether you are skimming along the waves or living the life of the undersea explorer, God's love for you is exactly the same. It never changes because He never changes.

If you are a wave-walker, keep an eye out for the hands of those reaching up from the depths. It may be a deep-sea explorer searching for the surface. You are God's hands, and that explorer may need your perspective.

If by chance you find yourself to be a deep-sea explorer, don't forget to look for treasure. The depths are full of sunken treasure that can be used on the surface. Don't miss the opportunity to gather today that which will be useful for tomorrow.

## Ponder and Pursue

In Romans 8:28, Paul said, "We know that God causes everything to work together for the good of those who love God and are called according to His purpose for them." God never changes. It doesn't matter if you are walking on the waves or exploring the depths of the sea—He is with you! He promised.

# DAY 68
## The Example

*"Keep putting into practice all you learned and received from me—everything you heard from me and saw me doing. Then the God of peace will be with you."*
*Philippians 4:9*

You are to be an example, but you are not *the* example. I was visiting with my daughter the other day, and we began to reminisce about the days when I had a day care service in my home. As a young mom, every now and again my daughter will call up and ask my thoughts on how a certain behavior or situation could be handled. As I have pondered her questions at different times, I am always honored that she sought out my thoughts and advice, even if she decides to go a different route.

Jesus said that if you have seen Him, you have seen the Father. Wow, that is quite the statement. Jesus was the perfect image of the Heavenly Father here on earth. Are you wondering what God thinks about a certain subject or situation? You can go to the Bible and see what Jesus said about it—then you will know what God thinks.

Unfortunately, I am not the perfect example. I have made plenty of mistakes, bad decisions, and oversights in my life. However, I have also made some good choices and recovered nicely from most of my mistakes. The Bible states that there is wisdom in a multitude of counselors.

Seek out those who have walked where you are going. They have gathered wisdom along the way, which could make your path smoother. Though I am not as bold as Paul, who says, "Put into practice *all* you have learned and received from me." I have gathered a few good suggestions over the years. I keep in mind that I am *an* example, but I am not *The Example*.

> **Ponder and Pursue**
>
> Follow The Example and be an example.

# DAY 69
## The Gardener

*"The LORD God placed the man in the Garden of Eden to tend and watch over it."*
*Genesis 2:15*

*"And some can pot begonias and some can bud a rose, and some are hardly fit to trust with anything that grows."*
*—Rudyard Kipling[15]*

I have often been accused of having a green thumb. I love to garden. I love to watch things grow. I get so excited about it that I grab whoever is around and take them on a tour of my garden, pointing out this new bloom and that new leaf. My family is very accommodating, and they have been on many tours.

One summer, I asked my son to come out to look at some newly bloomed flowers. After my little garden tour, my son told me he would never have a yard with flower beds, flowerpots, and grass to mow. No, it was too much work—nice to look at, but he didn't like all the labor involved. You can imagine the smile on my face when my son called from college one evening.

"Guess what I got today, Mom? I got a plant for my room. It has a really cool red bloom at the top, and it doesn't need direct sun." Don't you love that? He may have a garden bigger than mine someday.

God is the master gardener. He set Adam and Eve in the Garden of Eden to watch over and tend it. They were to watch it grow and do whatever it took to make that possible. It is the same for you today. God, your Father, the master gardener, placed you in your garden to watch over and tend it.

What is your garden? Your garden of influence consists of your family, friends, workplace, and church. Some of you don't want a garden because it is too much work. A nice garden takes effort and diligence. The benefit is worth it, though, as you are able to see harmony and blessing unfolding in the lives of those around you.

You will see growth in the people you have taken time with, encouraged, prayed for, and loved. You can then look to the Father and say, "Hey Dad, guess what I got for my room today? A plant with a cool red bloom on top." You, too, can get excited about gardening.

## Ponder and Pursue

Take a look at your garden today. Get excited about helping the people in your life grow and bloom into the beautiful image God has in mind for them.

# DAY 70
## The Great Exchange

*"This means that anyone who belongs to Christ has
become a new person. The old life is gone;
a new life has begun!"*
2 Corinthians 5:17

Several years ago, I attended a ladies' retreat located in a beautiful mountain getaway, complete with a river running through the property.

One of our activities was to write a situation or circumstance that was holding us back on a stick or a rock. Once that was completed, we were talk to God about our situation and ask for a new perspective.

Upon completion, we were to take the stick or rock and drop it over the edge of the bridge into the river and watch it float away. Then, to represent our new perspective, we were to find another rock, stick, or pinecone to take with us as a reminder.

This Great Exchange allowed us to let go of burdens and instead gain a new perspective. Only God can do that. He can take our old things and make them new.

> ### Ponder and Pursue
>
> Today I would like you to find rock or a stick and do your own Great Exchange, asking God to give you a new perspective.

## DAY 71
# The Lodestar Fixing our Gaze

*"Jesus Christ is the same yesterday, today, and forever."*
*Hebrews 13:8*

It is amazing how slowly time passes when you are trying to push through circumstances. As you reach certain milestones and look back, you realize the number of months that have passed. The very months seem to hold you captive one day at a time, barely allowing you to breathe. Moving forward also has its challenges.

When you are in such a struggle, it is hard to know which way is forward. Where am I going and how will I get there? Lewis Carroll, the author of *Alice in Wonderland*, offers this advice, "If you don't know where you are going, any road will get you there."[16]

While being caught in the swirling and churning of life's circumstances, you need to locate a lodestar, something that serves as a guide, or something on which your attention can be fixed.

For centuries, the North Star has been a lodestar for sailors. No matter the gravity of the storm, once the clouds begin to clear, the star is stable and unchanging. It offers a chance to get your bearings back and to determine the direction you were going before the storm. At that point, you can move forward or make basic changes to your itinerary or destination.

Hebrews 13:8 says, *"Jesus Christ is the same yesterday, today, and forever."* He is the perfect Lodestar—stable and unchanging. Keeping your focus on Christ will help you gain your bearings and start taking positive steps forward. You are urged in Colossians 3:2 to *"think about the things of heaven, not the things of earth."* Whatever you focus on, you will also empower.

Philippians 4:8 says, *"Finally, brothers and sisters, whatever is true, whatever is noble, whatever is right, whatever is pure, whatever is lovely, whatever is admirable—if anything is excellent or praiseworthy—think about such things."*

Now, while changing your thinking may not change your situation, it will give you the stability you need to make quality decisions, or to continue in your original direction with peace of mind. So, locate your Lodestar and move forward with confidence.

## Ponder and Pursue

Father, help me keep my mind and my focus on You today. I will think on that which is true, lovely and right. I thank You that You are the same yesterday, today and forever. Although my situations change, You remain stable. Thank You for being here with me.

## DAY 72
## The Lone Ranger

*"Two people are better off than one,
for they can help each other succeed."*
Ecclesiastes 4:9

I have a Lone Ranger toy from my childhood. Even though the TV shows were reruns from the black and white era, the Lone Ranger was still a superhero. He was fighting for justice and peace. The Lone Ranger was not really alone because he had his faithful companion, Tonto. Together they made an undefeatable duo.

Solomon, the writer of Ecclesiastes, states:

> *"Two people are better off than one, for they can help each other succeed. If one person falls, the other can*

*reach out and help. But someone who falls alone is in real trouble. Likewise, two people lying close together can keep each other warm. But how can one be warm alone? A person standing alone can be attacked and defeated, but two can stand back-to-back and conquer. Three are even better, for a triple-braided cord is not easily broken."* (Ecclesiastes 4:9-12)

Two are better than one. When you invest yourself in one another, you are investing in a mutual success. Companionship and accountability are staples of this human life. Sometimes you need someone to come alongside you, pick you up, protect you, and help you succeed.

Don't forget the last sentence of the verse: *Three are even better, for a triple-braided cord is not easily broken.* When you put Christ in the center of your relationships, you have a synergy that is not easily broken. You can become an undefeatable trio.

### Ponder and Pursue

Treasure your relationships today. Do you have a Tonto in your life, someone who has been there during the good and the bad? Make sure you are there for them today, too. Give them a call or send a text. You could even do something old-fashioned like sending a card in the mail.

# DAY 73
## The Map App

*"Trust in the LORD with all your heart; do not depend on your own understanding. Seek his will in all you do, and he will show you which path to take."*
*Proverbs 3:5-6*

A few years ago, our family had flown to the Washington, D.C. area for a wedding. My husband had arranged for a rental car, as did my sister-in-law. My husband borrowed a GPS to use on the trip, while my sister-in-law got one from the rental company.

The day after the wedding, we decided to visit downtown D.C. to see the sights. The traffic in Washington, D.C. is not for the faint of heart. As we approached the area, the traffic and endless construction were unbelievable. Even worse, our GPS was asking us to exit in places where there were no exits, not just once, but multiple times. The GPS never prompted us to take any of the available exits.

We drove long enough that we realized we were starting to pass the same construction zones we had been by earlier. Finally, we took a random exit and found ourselves driving on Massachusetts Avenue down Embassy Row.

Once we found parking downtown, we compared notes with my sister-in-law, who was following us on our long adventure around Washington, DC.

She asked, "Why didn't you take the exits the GPS told you to take?"

My husband replied, "They were all closed with construction."

It didn't take long to discover that the GPS my husband borrowed had not been updated for years, while my sister-in-law had the current one from the rental company. Needless to say, once the day was done, we followed my sister-in-law out of the city.

Sometimes it is hard to decide what exits to take in life, or if you should stay on the same road. Life is often complicated by unexpected roadblocks, careless people in your life, and pressures on all sides. There might even be sources of false or outdated information trying to direct you, like our outdated GPS. Making a decision with so many distractions going on can be difficult.

Our verse for today says that when you trust in God and seek His will for your life He will direct you. You also get direction from His word. Psalm 119:105 says, "Your word is a lamp to guide my feet and a light for my path." Filling yourself daily with His word and seeking His direction for your life will keep you updated.

There are also times you may need counsel to help make some of those big decisions. Proverbs 11:14 says, *"For lack of guidance a nation falls, but victory is won through many advisers."* Despite all the difficulties and pressures, seek God's direction for your life, fill yourself with His word, and seek counsel. Your destination is just ahead, and He is there to guide you.

### Ponder and Pursue

Pray, meditate, read the Word, and seek counsel. These are the things you need to stay updated in your life. When you fail to update, you will begin to experience glitches and gaps that could leave you wondering which way to go. Make sure you do your update today.

## DAY 74
## The Master Weaver

*"You saw me before I was born. Every day of my life was recorded in your book. Every moment was laid out before a single day had passed."*
Psalm 139:16

As you endure all the ups and downs of life's pathway, you may wonder, what is the purpose? Will my path ever be straight? Difficulties and hardships can make it all look so pointless.

The single thread of a tapestry cannot represent the full picture. You can often be caught up in a narrow line of vision, failing to see the whole picture. The Master Weaver knows every color of every thread; every weave is of a divine order. The finished product is not vague and sketchy in the mind of the weaver. He had a master plan before one thread went on the loom. Keep in mind the words of the Psalmist:

> *"You watched me as I was being formed in utter seclusion, as I was woven together in the dark of the womb. You saw me before I was born. Every day of my life was recorded in your book. Every moment was laid out before a single day had passed."* (Psalm 139:15-16)

The Master Weaver has plans and a purpose for your life. Look past the shadows in the tapestry and see the light—the glorious and breathtaking future He has for you.

---

### Ponder and Pursue

Widen your view today to catch a glimpse of all God has for you. His plan is glorious!

---

## DAY 75
## The Puzzle

*"God, pick up the pieces. Put me back together again.*
*You are my praise!"*
*Jeremiah 17:14[17]*

Remember the puzzle with one missing piece,
Beautiful yet incomplete?
Life can often feel that way,
Incomplete in many ways.
Troubles darken the corners of your life:
Hurt, anger, loneliness, strife.
But unlike the puzzle with one missing piece,
God can make our life complete.

Beautiful in every way,
God holds the pieces you need today.
Piece by piece, day by day,
You're beautiful and complete in every way.

### Ponder and Pursue

I pray for you today that you will find rest in God knowing that He holds all the pieces you need. Father, you will never leave us incomplete, for in You we are complete.

## DAY 76
## The Rose

*"It will be a shelter from daytime heat and a hiding place from storms and rain."*
Isaiah 4:6

The innocence of a rose,
It stands in perfect pose,
With very little strain,
It endures through the rain.

If we should stand so straight
In the storm, how would we rate?
Would we stand in perfect pose,
With the innocence of a rose?

## Ponder and Pursue

On your own you have very little to defend yourself against the storms of life. In our verse today, we see that God will provide our hiding place.

## DAY 77
## The Simple Becomes Profound

*"The human body has many parts, but the many parts make one whole body. So it is with the body of Christ."*
*1 Corinthians 12:12*

Music notes on a page are black and white. You can't feel them with the hand or the heart. Not until they are interpreted on an instrument do you get to experience the fullness and richness they hold.

One note by itself cannot express the beauty of the melody. However, when many notes are set together, they can gracefully express the most difficult arrangement. Working in harmony with one another, the simple becomes profound. Filling your senses and piercing your heart, the notes on a page come alive.

In the same way, you need to link arms and connect with those around you. Individually, you can make a sound. Collectively, our individual destiny and purpose will make the greatest impact. The simple becomes profound.

> ### Ponder and Pursue
>
> Are you connected today? Are you connected with people who can help accentuate who you are, while you are accentuating them? Together you will make the greatest impact.

# DAY 78
## The White Christmas Tree

*"The LORD is good to everyone.
He showers compassion on all his creation."
Psalm 145:9*

The empty nest is a very interesting time in a parent's life. It is a strange mix of newfound freedom and grieving over the loss of a long-lived era.

One of our Christmas traditions was to go into the forest and chop down a Christmas tree. Living on a mountain ranch made harvesting a Christmas tree an exciting and much-anticipated event. It also created two or three weeks of watering and picking up pine needles. I always told my children I was going to get an artificial tree once they stopped coming home for Christmas.

Well, that year eventually came, and both children were unable to come home for Christmas. I determined it was going to be the year of the artificial tree. Due to several unexpected expenses, I decided we should not spend money on an expensive "fake" tree. I even considered a Charlie Brown tree—one branch, one ornament, and good to go.

My husband came in one day for lunch with an old white Christmas tree that had been stored in the shop. He brought it over to put in the yard. However, I gave it a bath and put it in the living room. I strung it with colorful lights, pinecones I'd gathered from the yard, and nearly a dozen poinsettias I'd spent hours cutting out and gluing together.

There were several shocked (and a few horrified) people over my well-used, somewhat abused white Christmas tree. I enjoyed the tree, including cleaning it up, straightening the crumpled branches, and hand-picking each ornament.

In some strange way, I think that little tree and I had some things in common. We were both a little frazzled and definitely imperfect. Like the tree, I was living a whole new life scenario and feeling a little inadequate. But we were both standing straight and tall, trying to radiate the light and beauty that is resident only because of the grace and mercy of God.

## Ponder and Pursue

Are you in a season where life is taking some unexpected turns? Choose to look on the bright side of things. Yes, I said "choose." Every day, you decide how you will feel and react to situations around you. Maybe you are in a white Christmas tree season—if so, decorate it with all your might and a little creativity.

## DAY 79
## Those Little Foxes

*"Catch all the foxes, those little foxes, before they ruin the vineyard of love, for the grapevines are blossoming!"*
*Song of Solomon 2:15*

In our scripture today, the little foxes were destroying the vineyard. Ground squirrels and mice are smaller but just as destructive.

I love spending time in my garden. Each new bloom refreshes me, and I find fulfillment in the nurturing process. A good gardener keeps watch over her plants, looking for unhealthy leaves and pests of any kind. Can you believe that ground squirrels and mice fall into the pest category? In my garden, they do.

Because they are sneaky, these rodents don't always go right for the stem or the leaves. Often, they tunnel underground and eat the roots. By the time you notice the wilted leaves, there is usually not much left of the plant to nurture.

Beware of the little rodents that can spoil your life—the negative attitudes and actions that work just under the surface. It is those little things that slowly destroy your roots, your life-giving source.

> ### Ponder and Pursue
>
> Watch for those attitudes and actions that will choke the life out of you. Don't allow them to stay. Pay attention, be quick and be aggressive. Remember, "It is the little foxes that spoil the vine."

## DAY 80
### Throw in the Towel

*"Fight the good fight for the true faith. Hold tightly to the eternal life to which God has called you, which you have confessed so well before many witnesses."*
*1 Timothy 6:12*

When my son was in karate tournaments, I was one of the moms who sat ringside and kept time for the match. When time was up, I threw in the towel. That meant time was up—hands and feet to yourself.

There is a right time to throw in the towel and a wrong time. We might find ourselves growing tired before the time is up, or maybe that last punch hurt a little too much. But we need to keep pressing on, never giving up.

Refocus on your training, get your blocks in, and throw a few kicks. Don't panic, remember your instructors' voice, and persevere. Do you see the parallel between the karate match and life?

> ### Ponder and Pursue
>
> Don't throw in the towel too early. Never give up—keep your focus and rely on God's word.

## DAY 81
## Time to Get Up

*"Anyone who belongs to God listens to the words of God."*
*John 8:47a*

Years ago, after high school graduation, our daughter went on an organized mission trip to Brazil that included ministry and community outreach opportunities. One morning while she was there, I awoke around 4:00 a.m. with a sudden urge call her.

After several minutes of struggling back and forth with the idea, now unable to sleep, I decided to call. I thought I might have missed her as the phone continued to ring. Suddenly, a sleepy voice answered the phone. "Good morning," I said to her. "I woke up a while ago thinking of you and wanted to call and say hi."

There was a moment of silence while she pondered my statement.

She then asked what time it was, realizing that she had over slept. Her alarm had not gone off, and the outreach bus was scheduled to leave in a few minutes. Her next comment stood out to me more than any other: "Next time, call me as soon as you think of it—I would have had more time."

Even though her alarm didn't go off, God woke me up 5,000 miles away to be her alarm. I almost talked myself out of it. If I had, she would have missed her outreach or caused the entire group to be late. God wanted to give her thirty minutes; my delay only gave her ten.

It is sometimes easy to dismiss God when He is speaking. In this situation, I tried to talk myself out of calling because it seemed silly. God gently nudges us sometimes, and if we don't learn to give attention to these promptings, we could miss something He has for us, or for us to do.

### Ponder and Pursue

Can you think of some gentle nudges that God has spoken to your heart? Did you act on these or let them slide by? We all have our list of the nudges we chose not to heed.

Take a moment to write down one or two that caused you to take action. Think about how God spoke to your heart and the result of your obedience.

# DAY 82
## To Spank or Not to Spank

*"Do not judge others, and you will not be judged."*
*Matthew 7:1*

As young parents, there are so many decisions to consider. Breast milk or formula, cloth or disposable diapers, let them cry or snuggle them to sleep? What about: to spank or not to spank, organic or non-organic, store bought baby food or home-made, to raise your voice or not to raise you voice? The list just goes on and on.

How could one little fella come with so many choices attached? And that is the tip of the iceberg. As they grow, there is the question of public school, private school, or homeschool. How high can the skirt be, or how low can the top be?

I am not going to answer any of those questions today. I do, however, want to make a point. No matter what choices you make, someone you know will make the opposite choice. What you don't want to do is alienate each other with your parenting styles. Don't judge a formula mom because you are a breast-feeding mom, or criticize the homeschooling mom because you feel her children will be social misfits.

You need to support each other. There is no manual for raising the perfect kid with the perfect parenting style. In fact, a parenting style may not work well twice in the same family. Don't be harsh and judgmental of your peers. Everyone is trying to do the very best job possible.

### Ponder and Pursue

Encourage, encourage, encourage. You are pouring your hearts into this job of parenting. Encourage someone today who may be feeling a little overwhelmed and needs a pat on the back.

## DAY 83
## *Treasured*

*"My sheep listen to my voice; I know them,
and they follow me."*
*John 10:27*

My husband's grandmother was an amazingly talented woman. She could sing, play piano, paint scenery, or sketch a portrait. She could tap dance and even walk on her hands. However, the things she took the most joy in were her children and grandchildren.

She cherished every moment spent with her loved ones. She never wanted you to leave when you came to visit, and saying goodbye on the phone was a chore. She longed for your presence and treasured the very sound of your voice.

God, our Heavenly Father, cherishes every moment you spend

with Him, and treasures the very sound of your voice. Do you treasure the sound of your Father's voice? Do you long to be in His presence? Are you so saturated in His love that every moment spent with Him is as precious as the very air you breathe?

If not, let's start cultivating it today. Recognize God's presence is always with you, He loves you with a never-ending love. You are the apple of His eye. You are His bride, His beloved. Wrap yourself in His gentle arms. Be soothed by the peace in His voice. You will find yourself longing for His presence, being saturated with His love.

### Ponder and Pursue

"Father, I thank You for loving us beyond measure. I pray that we will long for Your presence in our lives, just like a grandma yearning for her loved ones. Help us to recognize Your voice as You call to us and whisper our names."

## DAY 84
## Valentine's Day

*"Why am I discouraged? Why is my heart so sad? I will put my hope in God! I will praise him again—my Savior and my God!"*
*Psalm 42:11*

Valentine's Day is a day of love, affection, and romance. One year, my husband surprised me with a breakfast date before church. It is a special treat for us to leave a little early on a Sunday morning and head for our favorite restaurant for delicious blue corn waffles and breakfast enchiladas. Of course, we split our plates so we each could have the best of both worlds.

As we pulled into our small mountain town, we noticed things didn't seem quite normal. Usually, the streets are abuzz with skiers and winter tourists heading for the slopes, the nearest coffee shop, or a restaurant.

On that day, there was hardly a soul in sight. We also noticed all the shops on the main street were closed. It was a power outage. The power had been out all night, and the crews were still working to remedy the situation.

Our much-anticipated breakfast date was now taking on a different look. We decided to go to the market and see if they were running on a generator. Sure enough, they had power, but the food at the deli's hot bar was completely gone. It was the only place in town to get hot food. While waiting in line at the deli, the man ahead of us asked if they would be replenishing the food on the hot bar.

"No, you should have been here yesterday" the clerk replied.

The man just stood there looking puzzled.

Finally, the clerk said, "You will have to come back tomorrow."

Somewhat in amusement and disbelief at the confusing and rude comments of the deli attendant, we wandered off to get a protein drink and granola bars.

You are often challenged by situations and circumstances that threaten your plans, attitudes, and outlooks. You are seldom in control of those situations, but you are in control of your attitudes. Yes, I was disappointed that I missed out on my delicious breakfast, but it did not affect my attitude or the outlook for my day.

As we sat in the parking lot eating our granola bars and protein drinks, we decided that Plan B was working out okay. It was not our Plan A, but we were together, and that was what mattered.

> ### Ponder and Pursue
>
> If you are living in Plan B today, do it with a joyful heart. You can't always change circumstances, but you can change your attitudes.

# DAY 85
# Valentine's Day, The Saga Continues

*"Casting down imaginations, and every high thing that exalteth itself against the knowledge of God, and bringing into captivity every thought to the obedience of Christ."*
*2 Corinthians 10:5[18]*

Due to a Valentine's Day power outage, our breakfast date turned out to be granola bars and a protein drink in the privacy of our SUV parked in the market parking lot. After our market date, we went on to church.

When we arrived, we realized that our church heating system was dependent on electricity. Since the power had been out all night, the sanctuary was quite chilly. In fact, several people still had on their beanies and winter coats, and there were even a few blankets here and there.

Our worship service was unplugged, but the message was the same length as usual. There were several little icebergs filling the sanctuary chairs.

After the service was over, we decided to join some friends and go to a neighboring town for a nice warm lunch. After a great lunch and a wonderful time with our friends, we headed home.

The evening was growing late as I enjoyed my quite time before bed. Suddenly, a loud spray of water coming from our kitchen interrupted the quiet. I jumped up and ran to the kitchen to find water running rapidly from under the refrigerator. I realized the hose to the icemaker must have come off.

My mind racing, I ran in and woke my husband. I hurried back to the kitchen, tugging on the refrigerator to pull it out far enough that I could squeeze between the refrigerator and the wall. I soon found myself lying over the counter, hanging off the edge to reach the valve—mission accomplished. Only now, I was stuck between the wall and the refrigerator, hanging upside down off the edge of the counter.

My husband came to the rescue and pulled me out of my predicament. After much mopping and moving of furniture, everything was cleaned up. Repairs could be done the next day.

Once again, we are often challenged by situations and circumstances that threaten our plans, attitudes, and outlooks. I had no control over the temperature in the church sanctuary, nor did I have control over the water hose on our icemaker coming off and flooding our kitchen and utility room.

I did have control over my attitude. I had the choice to let these circumstances control me, or gain control over them by maintaining control over myself. This Valentine's Day was a lesson—not on love, affection, or romance, but on self-control.

> ### Ponder and Pursue
>
> Take charge of your attitude and watch the situations and circumstances of this world lose their grip on you.

## DAY 86

# What Is My Father Doing?

*"So Jesus explained, "I tell you the truth, the Son can do nothing by himself. He does only what he sees the Father doing. Whatever the Father does, the Son also does."*
*John 5:19*

As my husband and I prepared to visit our children in Virginia, we decided to purchase a new mattress for their guest room. The mattress was one of the new memory-foam mattresses that could be shipped in a box, and when unrolled, it would magically turn into a full-size mattress.

Our daughter videoed the unwrapping of the mattress and emailed it to us. We watched our son-in-law work to de-box and unwrap the mattress from its plastic-wrap cocoon. We got such enjoyment watching our then 11-month-old grandson trying to be just like Daddy. Crawling over to be near, he began tugging, pounding, and mimicking his dad the best he could.

I watched our little guy's efforts and could see his feelings of accomplishment. I began to think of my relationship with my Heavenly Father. Jesus said that He only did what He saw the Father doing and said what He heard the Father saying.

Just like my grandson, you need to diligently watch the Father, and do what He is doing and say what He is saying. Will you be perfect? Probably not. However, as you grow in your efforts, you will one day be able to unwrap the box just like Daddy.

> **Ponder and Pursue**
>
> "Lord, help me be just like you."

## DAY 87

# What's Their Name, Mommy?

*"But now, O Jacob, listen to the LORD who created you. O Israel, the one who formed you says, "Do not be afraid, for I have ransomed you. I have called you by name; you are mine."*
*Isaiah 43:1*

When our grandson was two years old he discovered that all people had a name, and most had a middle name and a last name. One day while visiting on FaceTime, he asked, "Nana, what is your middle name?" I was shocked that he even knew what a middle name was.

He wanted to know everyone's name, including strangers walking down the street, the guy who helped clean up an "oops" at the grocery store, and even random cartoon characters. Unfortunately, my daughter and son-in-law do not know everyone's name, much to the disappointment of our grandson.

Even though you don't know everyone's name, and probably don't really care to, God does. He knows you by name. Our scripture today says, "I have called you by name; you are mine."

Doesn't it feel good to walk into a frequently visited business and have the clerk call you by name and greet you? You feel a part of something. You feel known and maybe even special. While you don't know everyone, God does. He has called you by name.

### Ponder and Pursue

Write your name on a sticky note. After your name, place a comma and write the words: "I have called you by name; you are mine." Put that sticky note on your bathroom mirror and read it out loud every morning this week.

## DAY 88

## Who Are You? Peacock or Chameleon?

*"Therefore, accept each other just as Christ has accepted you so that God will be given glory."*
Romans 15:7

Who are you? Are you like a peacock? They stand out in the crowd. They are flamboyant and hard to miss. This fun, outgoing personality isn't a bad thing. Confidence, creativity, and determination will often launch a peacock onto the stage of success.

Maybe you are like a chameleon that blends in. They are the background people. Chameleons are generally loyal, reserved, detailed, and dedicated. Chameleons are great support and keep everything running smoothly backstage.

The strength of a peacock can be intimidating to the more laid-back personality of a chameleon. The peacocks need to bathe their confidence in kindness and consideration, never running over others to achieve their goal. They should also search out the chameleons in their lives that have blended into the wallpaper and pull them out for a moment of gratitude.

The chameleons, on the other hand, can blend in so much that their identity disappears. They are always Jack's wife, or Sally's mom, Emily's husband, or that guy who works with Bob. If the chameleon is not secure in who they are, they can begin to compare themselves to the peacock.

This comparison can bring a wide range of conflicting feelings: inadequacy, annoyance, and jealousy. But what most chameleons don't recognize is that the peacock needs encouragement. They seem to run well on their own steam; however, they need to be encouraged and appreciated like everyone else.

Chameleons and peacocks both need to be confident about who they are and what they do without being inconsiderate or unkind. Did you notice the peacock and the chameleon need to be encouraged and acknowledged? Both may walk through life looking and acting differently, but we all need each other.

Chameleons can offer some order and peace to the life of a peacock. The peacock can add a little sparkle and energy to the life of a chameleon. Perhaps the peacock will add enough sparkle to see through the chameleon's camouflage.

## Ponder and Pursue

Are you a peacock or a chameleon? Be confident in who you are. Don't fall into the trap of wishing you were someone else, or judging someone because they are different. Embrace how we are all uniquely designed.

# DAY 89
## Wrinkle Remover

*"He did this to present her to himself as a glorious church without a spot or wrinkle or any other blemish. Instead, she will be holy and without fault."*
Ephesians 5:27

In today's world, we are bombarded with every beauty tip, suggestion, and high-priced miracle cream on the market. Everything from purified water, melon extracts, and coconut oil is going to rid us of wrinkles and dark spots. At least, that is our hope.

As a young girl, I remember thinking how pretty my grandma was. She had worked hard all her young life picking cotton and working in the garden. She worked in a bomb plant during World War II. She and my grandpa married and started a family during the Great Depression. However, you would never know by looking at her that she had labored so hard during her life.

The beauty I saw in my Grandma was not that she had or didn't have any wrinkles. As a little girl, I truly don't remember any wrinkles or dreaded dark spots. What I do remember is the smiling lady dressed in her 1950's-style dress, greeting me with a smile and a hug. She always made me feel special.

I remember her working in the garden in her jeans, over-sized hat, and sweatshirt. But when we were going to go to town she had to hurry in and "put on her face" before we could leave.

My grandma's beauty was in her attitude. When you look at life through the eyes of hope and expectation, those around you will see that life reflecting in your face. Even though the only miracle cream you would see on my grandma's counter was a little white jar of Pond's Cold Cream, she was radiant with love for her family.

> ### Ponder and Pursue
>
> If you are ready to order the newest miracle-working wrinkle remover, consider your attitude first. Truly, your outlook on life will have the greatest impact on how people see you.

# DAY 90
## What Is Your Passion?

*"But I have raised you up for this very purpose, that I might show you my power and that my name might be proclaimed in all the earth."*
*Exodus 9:16[19]*

What is your passion? My husband has been asking this question repeatedly in the messages he shares from the pulpit, the posts on his Facebook page, and his everyday conversations. What is your passion, and are you pursuing it?

I must admit, I don't know for sure. Yes, just because my husband is the passion preacher doesn't mean I have it figured out for myself yet, although I am working on it. Life is so full of change. Sometimes that change leaves you wondering what the next step is.

My passion for the past thirty-something years has been my family. I have been focused on being the best wife, mother, and homeschool teacher I can be. Now that life has moved on and roles are changing, I am left wondering what my answer is to my husband's question. What is my passion and am I pursuing it?

I have always liked to write. Is it my passion? I seem to go through seasons of writing every day or so, then nothing for weeks or even months. But I do have many articles, thoughts, devotions, and poems all written out and stored on my computer. It seemed like to a good idea to organize them and make a devotional book. I quickly found out that I was in over my head with organizing, editing, and trying to figure out the amazing online publishing platform. HELP!

Why did I think this would be a good idea? My motivation quickly slipped away. I told my husband of my serious lack of motivation.

"If nothing else, you should pursue it as a gift for the children. They would treasure the ramblings of their mother," he said.

A light flickered on. I am not the visionary, planning to reach the multitudes with my little devotional. However, I can get excited about putting together all my writings for my children and grandchildren. My passion is and always has been family. I am not trying to reach the multitudes, but if I do, we will know that God is a miracle working God.

My passion is fulfilled as I share what God has done in my life with my friends, family, children, and grandchildren. A chuckle, a memory, and maybe even a tear, and we will remember that God is always faithful. I hope you guys have enjoyed this little book. Maybe you will even want to read it again some time.

One more thing: what is your passion and are you pursuing it?

# Conclusion

Reflecting through our time together, I trust that you could catch a glimpse of how God can move in your daily life.

As you prepare to close this book I pray that you will be established in hope and focused on God.

Enjoy the Journey!

*Theresa*

## About the Author:

Theresa Cannon's authentic and practical approach will encourage you to recognize God in your daily life. From the days of disappointment to finally reaching the top of your mountain, you will see that God has traveled with you every step of the journey.

Theresa and her husband David have been married over 30 years. She is the mother of two and delights in being a grandmother. Theresa's journey includes being raised by an amazing single mom, finding faith as a young adult, and marrying the man of her dreams.

On her journey, she found herself stepping into the uncertain waters of parenthood and homeschooling for seventeen years.

These days she is navigating the empty nest stage of life. Faith, family, friends and flowers are the heartbeat of Theresa's life.

Theresa and her husband, David, are both authors and have ministered together for over 30 years. Theresa is a Certified Christian Life Coach, Biblical Counselor, Prepare/Enrich Facilitator, Author and Speaker.

TheresaCannon.org

# WANT TO WORK WITH *Theresa Cannon?*

Theresa is a Certified Christian Life Coach, Biblical Counselor, Prepare/Enrich Facilitator, Author and Speaker.

To connect with Theresa, visit her website at TheresaCannon.org.

Invite Theresa and David Cannon to your next event:
David and Theresa are available for ministry engagements such as:

- Conferences
- Workshops
- Trainings
- Seminars

Topics include:

- Healing
- Learning to Hear God
- Marketplace Ministry
- Dreams and Dream Interpretation
- Pre-Married and Marriage seminars
- Relationship Strategies and much more.

Theresa's husband, David Cannon, is also an author, teacher, and pastor, and ministers in the prophetic.

To find out more about David and to purchase his book, **God Speaks Recognizing the Voice,** visit: www.DavidCannonMinistries.com.

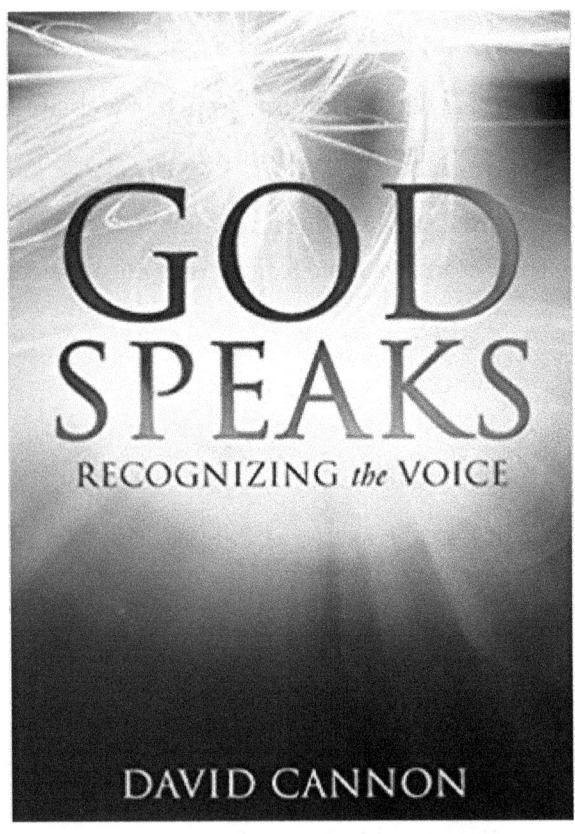

# Endnotes

[1]*New International Version, Biblehub.com*, Biblehub, 2016, 11 May 2017 <http://biblehub.com/psalms/17-8.htm>

[2]Wikipedia contributors, "Apple of my eye," *Wikipedia, The Free Encyclopedia*, 13 Mar 2017, Web, 11 May 2017 <https://en.wikipedia.org/w/index.php?title=Apple_of_my_eye&oldid=770130810>

[3]*King James Version, Biblehub.com*, Biblehub, 2016, 11 May 2017 <http://biblehub.com/psalms/23-6.htm>

[4]*King James Version, Biblehub.com*, Biblehub, 2016, 11 May 2017 <http://biblehub.com/2_corinthians/10-5.htm>

[5]*King James Version, Biblehub.com*, Biblehub, 2016, 11 May 2017 <http://biblehub.com/2_corinthians/1-5.htm>

[6]King, Hobart, "Diamond-Gem and Industrial Uses-Mineral Properties," 2017, *Geology.com*, 7 March 2017 <http://geology.com/minerals/diamond.shtml>

[8]Trex, Ethan, "10 People Who Switched Careers After 50 (and Thrived!)," *Mental Floss*, 22 January 2016, Web, 13 March 2017 <http://mentalfloss.com/article/24688/10-people-who-switched-careers-after-50-and-thrived>

[9]Wikipedia contributors, "Ray Kroc," *Wikipedia, The Free Encyclopedia*, 9 May 2017, Web, 13 March 2017 <https://

en.wikipedia.org/wiki/Ray_Kroc>

[10] Chery, Fritz, "25 Encouraging Bible Verses About Old Age,"

*27 July 2017, Bible Reasons*, 13 March 2017 <http://www.whatchristianswanttoknow.com/bible-verses-about-strength-25-encouraging-scripture-quotes/>

[11]*New International Version, Biblehub.com*, Biblehub, 2016, 11 May 2017 <http://biblehub.com/proverbs/10-6.htm>

[12]*King James Version, Biblehub.com*, Biblehub, 2016, 11 May 2017 <http://biblehub.com/hebrews/3-13.htm>

[13]*New International Version, Biblehub.com*, Biblehub, 2016, 11 May 2017 <http://biblehub.com/2_corinthians/9-8.htm>

[14]*New International Version, Biblehub.com*, Biblehub, 2016, 11 May 2017 <http://biblehub.com/deuteronomy/5-33.htm>

[15]Kipling, Rudyard, "The Glory of the Garden," *Poems—The Glory of the Garden*, 14 March 2017 <http://www.kiplingsociety.co.uk/poems_garden.htm>

[16]Lewis Carroll," BrainyQuote.com, Xplore Inc, 2017, 10 May 2017 <https://www.brainyquote.com/quotes/quotes/l/lewiscarro165865.html>

[17]*The Message Bible, BibleGateway.com*, Zondervan, 2008, 11 May 2017 <https://www.biblegateway.com/passage/?search=jeremiah+7%3A14&version=MSG>

[18]*King James Version, Biblehub.com*, Biblehub, 2016, 11 May 2017 <http://biblehub.com/2_corinthians/10-5.htm>

[19]*New International Version, Biblehub.com*, Biblehub, 2016, 11 May 2017 <http://biblehub.com/exodus/9-16.htm>

All references are taken from the New Living Translation unless otherwise noted within the chapters.

www.ingramcontent.com/pod-product-compliance
Lightning Source LLC
Chambersburg PA
CBHW051823090426
42736CB00011B/1621